Authors Note

My first words are to thank the 100 or so sponsors who believed in this project enough to invest in it and make this local and independent initiative accessible to all.

Thank you everyone.

There have been times when I have deliberated with my conscience a[illegible] I have been writing this book. For publicising this beautiful piece of English countryside may increase the numbers of people visiting an area with an inadequate infrastructure to welcome them. Nevertheless, we are about to enter a new era, that of the 21st. century and indications are there will be an ever increasing rhythm of change to almost everything we know. Thus education and understanding now becomes the major motivation for producing this booklet, in hope that those who live on and visit the Blackdowns will have a better understanding of this place and how to perceive it.

The Blackdown Hills are truly an island to themselves being geographically removed to 300 meters above a hive of industry and human activity in the valley floors which surround them. Steep inclines up the escarpments, and a wild reputation have protected the land and the people from irascible change through many centuries. Some would say The Blackdowns are a historical icon for sanctuary and solitude, in a world that, 'Has progressively gone quite mad'.

As we approach the Millennium we find that this island, not unlike many others in this modern age, has become smaller and less resilient to change. The new A303, the first privately funded road construction in this country since the 18th century, may cut a great swathe through The Blackdowns from Honiton to Ilminster, in spite of the Blackdowns being declared an Area of Outstanding Natural Beauty. Even more sinister and subtle is the decline in the economic survival of small farms and the traditional industries essential to the maintenance of the landscape and country way of life. The knowledge and skills that have determined the shape of this landscape over the centuries, for the first time is no longer guaranteed to be passed on from generation to generation.

Therefore, it seems all the more essential for those who live in the Blackdowns to be able to acquaint themselves with a knowledge of the services, opportunities and [illegible]ment around them. A place where well informed peo[illegible] utilise each other's skills towards good ste[illegible] balanced social and economic e[illegible]ging world. If there has been any [illegible] & Guide, then this notion must [illegible]t to turn villages into hosts of [illegible] rather, to provide a printed [illegible] and businesses exist, at the [illegible]overy and recreation.

[illegible] may have shared the same doubts and aspirations for [illegible] as myself, when he penned his book 'Unknown Somerset' in 1927. That of fear for impending changes and something irretrievably lost. Perhaps like me, he chose to believe that ignorance and poor perceptions were the greatest enemies of a delicate environment and chose to write about what he found here, in hope that his words might bring it protection.

Happy is the country that has no history, and happier still is the countryside that has no popular attractions. Beyond the monument to the Iron Duke, an obelisk that stands upon the heights above Wellington, there is nothing about the Blackdown Hills of such an obvious nature that scores of thousands of people in chara-a-bancs must flock to see it. Consequently you may roam about, even in the holiday of mid August,and find lanes almost deserted and shady glades of woodland without even picnics and come upon little farms and secluded homesteads nestling under the long ridge - a ridge that is dark with pine and mountain ash .

Donald Maxwell .
'Unknown Somerset', 1927 .

The Blackdown Hills
Northern Road Maps

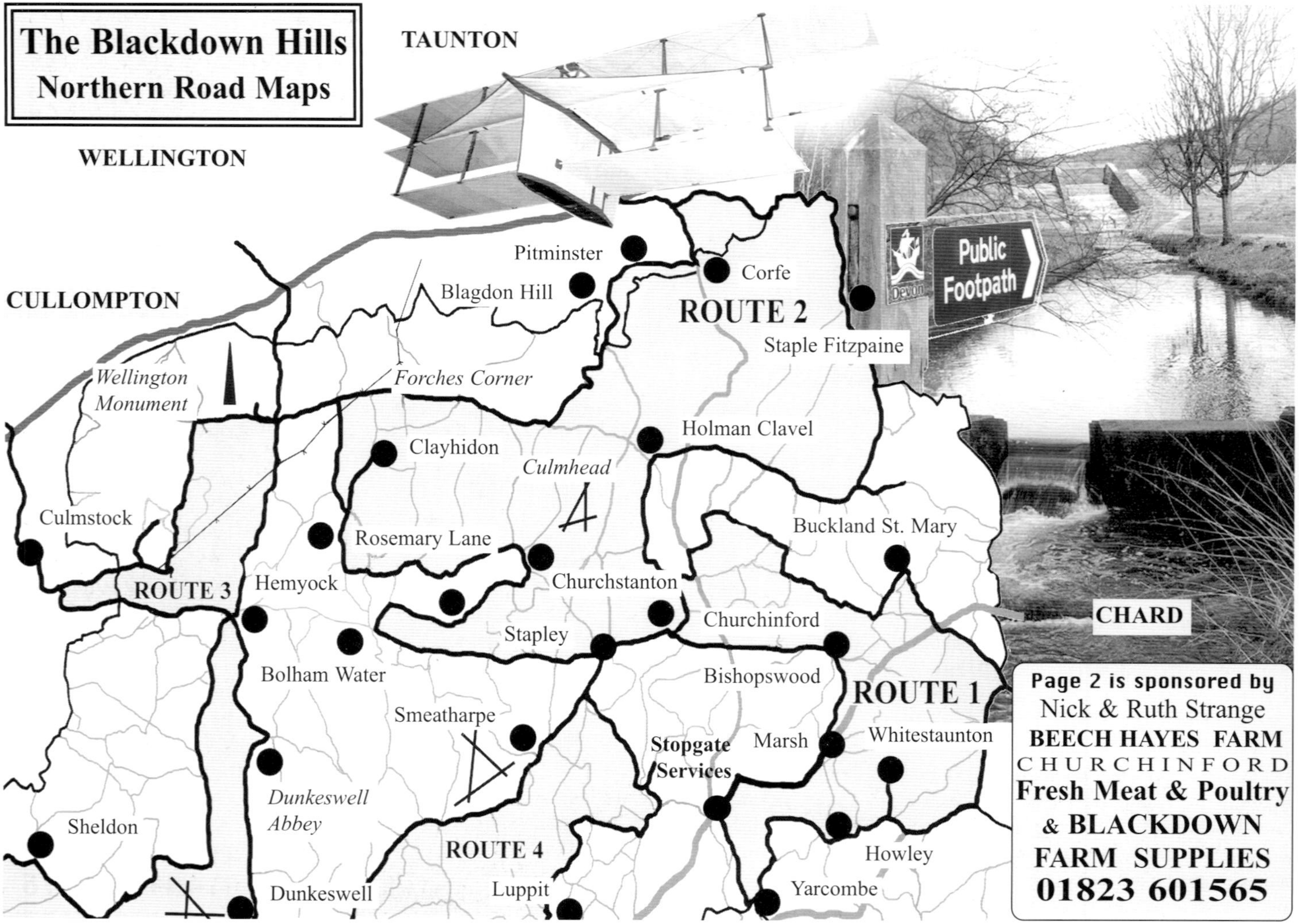

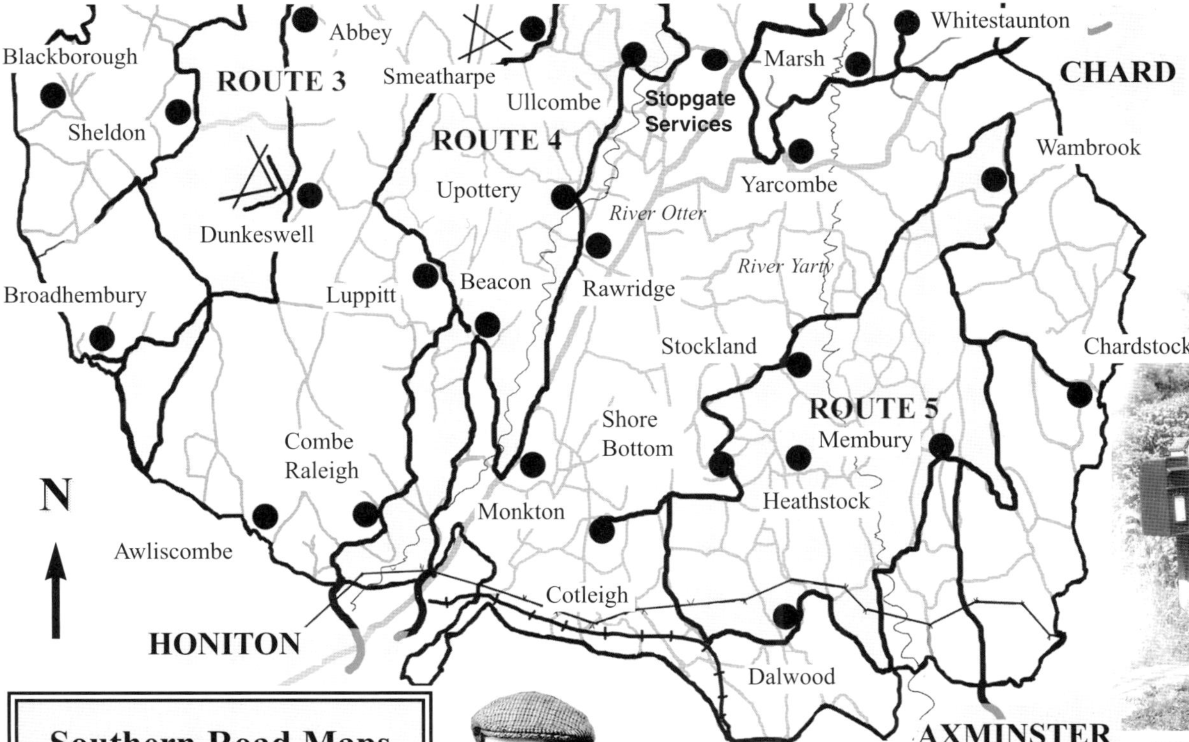

Southern Road Maps

THE HANDBOOK AND CONTENTS

The Handbook divides the Blackdown Area of Outstanding Natural Beauty into 5 main Routes of discovery with an overview in the front and a directory to social activities, services and businesses in the back.

NOTES ON THIS PUBLICATION

Whilst the authors of this book have made every effort to describe accurately the short walks, rides and routes in this book, they cannot guarantee that these rights of way will be in good condition, or be accessible to the traveller. Our diagrams are intended only as impressions of routes and for more detailed cartography, you should refer to Ordinance Survey publications. Whilst every attempt has been made to provide the directories with accurate information, without infringing privacy or rights to information, the authors, distributors and publishers accept no legal responsibility for misinformation or data passed onto them from other bodies.

The Real Lords of the Blackdowns

The great buzzard stretched and arched his left wing to spill the weight of the warm Widcombe air skillfully through the black brown feathers of his wing tips. 'Not too much!' Just enough to angle his body over the leafy crowns of the great avenue of beech trees edging the lush green meadow. The self same meadow which gives birth to the river Culm.
'Good'! He had judged this breeze well, even with the uplift on the heat radiating from the vast mantle of green spring fresh leaves.
'That's the trick, let the thermals do the work'!
The great bird kept almost every muscle motionless, only to turn his head a little towards his target and blink a skin lidded reptilian eye to clear his vision as he cleared the canopy.
'Just about there'. - 'That's it! There's that small blade of grass working against the rhythm of the breeze!'
The great wall of beech trees had hidden his approach. The distance travelled to and travelled from first sighting had been computed totally blind. He straightened his wings a little more, spilling air to glide inches over the seed heads of the long summer grass. Suddenly he braked hard, stalling to hover for a second and then, as his talons found the little field mouse, his wings folded around the little death in an exaggerated dipping curtain.
The great bird felt the little body succumb and give its life to him beneath the weight of his talons. The genes of a thousand ancestors had made him the great hunter. Those of the tiny rodent the ready sacrifice each equally essential to life on the greensand plain of the Blackdowns.
Once, when time was less old the ancient upthrust seabed was flat and characterless. A great salt sea lapped high up the Northern escarpments. A succession of frosts and hot summer suns gradually weathered the surface and water started to cut pathways into the weakest sand. The valleys widened as the run off and seep carried the plateaux away into the deepening Culm, Yarty, Otter and Five Head rivers, each to forge winding paths to a slowly receding sea. The valley sides and the ancient cliffs to become the engines for the thermals making flight so effortless for the Lord of the Blackdowns.

Times were, when bear, wild boar, great cats, mammoth and even rhinoceros roamed the endless tracts of dog oak, furze, and mountain ash which flourished here. Lichens and mosses covered the dense forest surrounding the peat bogs, where stoat, weasel, fox, wolf and a hundred other small creatures competed for life. Some species to become extinct but not the great buzzards. Even when man first put tentative steps onto the Blackdowns, even with the ‘Two Leg’s' quirky habits for setting fires to hunt his prey, he helped the buzzard as he created clearings and later meadows for agriculture, developing habitats well suited to catching small game with easily accessible, trees for nesting.
Change has come. Yet, much of the woodland still survives. The buzzard thrives here despite the threats from pesticides, insecticides and fungicides. Somehow the shape of the land hasn't made these atrocities so financially viable here. For a short time at least, the Lords of the Blackdowns are secure and thriving, with nearly a pair per half mile, on the high escarpments.

Trends and Changes

"With every single human footfall comes change to some small piece of the World. There are so many of us humans now that we must seriously consider the implications of our presence within the confines of a global environment. One that suffers greatly from our modern lifestyles. How do we encourage a universal consciousness for preserving the 'Natural World', when we are so excited and mesmerised by our own creation? That of the electronic universe - The Global Village!"

The Author in an Internet conversation with the media guru, Naom Chomskey 1997.

Environments such as the Blackdown Hills are very precious. They echo that there is still left a small island of English countryside which is not yet lost to the motor car, urbanisation and technological mayhem. Even so, the landscape is under threat from irreversible change.

It can be argued that the beauty found here is not the total result of nature. More likely, it is nature moulded by a continuous, mostly harmonious relationship between it and the farmer over centuries of challenge. If this is the case, then perhaps we should consider very seriously how the beauty of the landscape can be maintained by countrywise stewards, whilst modern economic pressures dictate that farms have to be large and efficient to provide abundant, standardised supermarket products. Agri-chemicals and the grubbing out of ancient hedgerows do not embrace the preservation of wild creatures, or the indigenous plant life to be found on the Blackdown greensand geology. The very backbone of the Blackdowns, those small ecologically friendly farms are ceasing to exist because they are no longer economically viable. It seems increasingly difficult therefore, to envision that this ancient landscape can be maintained without being subsidised from those who live here or from outside sources.

Many farm houses and barnyards have become the property of those who can afford to escape the gridlock and unease of our towns and cities. The attractions for living here are a clean environment, quaint architecture and opportunities for rural leisure, all within a short distance of getting to work on a motorway. However, the new age country dweller's expectations for country living can differ greatly from those of the country person who's family has lived here for centuries.

The Blackdown Hills were designated an Area of Outstanding Natural Beauty in July 1993. Strategy plans and regulations attempt to find solutions. However, for these to be successful, ideas need to be generated willingly from those who live here; with a view to maintaining a durable economy whilst keeping the area environmentally sound. Top down regulation might well destroy the very thing that conservationists are trying to protect. The environment is important here but no more so than the livelihoods of the families who work the area, are intuitive to its needs and promote the country way of life. In a perfect world there would be space for non chemical, non intensive farming methods where produce from the Blackdowns would become trusted by consumers as guaranteed healthy, free from chemicals and branded as such. Any chances of this happening seem slim with present Common Agricultural Policies. Yet, if the traditional farmer can no longer afford to exist here into the future, then the area and what it has to offer is in serious jeopardy!

Early human links with the Blackdowns

Hundreds of thousands of years of weathering has exposed flint rock and cherts to lie in the top soils. Over a period of time man learnt to shape and design these sharp stones into his early tools and weapons, well before the Mesolithic period (c 8000 - 4000 BC) and that of the Neolithic period, (c 4000 - 2000 BC). Because of this, the Blackdowns became a very important centre of human activity during those periods, perhaps much more so than now. Archeological finds through limited field work in the upper Yarty Valley and at Hembury Fort suggest, that much of the Blackdown Plateaux may have been inhabited at that time. Perhaps giving some credence to the ancient folk tales that there was once a great city high on the high Blackdown plateaux.

By the beginning of the bronze age (c 2000 - 800 BC) many of the forest trees had been cleared by the bronze age people, who's numerous round burial barrows are known to have dotted the tops of the plateaux. Some still survive (Robin Hoods Butts) and can be seen to this day. Pathways criss crossed valley floors and good tracks ran to make a complex infrastructure along the length of ridge tops, where goods could be back packed or sled transported for trade in some safety.

A people came to the hill forts who made beaker shaped pottery (The Beaker People). Others came to this place who were skilled in making leather and smelting and shaping bronze into tools and armoury. By then oxen were used to carry loads and to pull ploughs to create cultivated fields down the valley sides, adjacent to the safety of the hill top forts. Homes were built inside a palisade of sharp pointed barricades, made of mud and stone with thatchings of brackens and grasses, placed over wooden beams. Fresh water fish would have been abundant in the deep river valleys of the Culm, Yarty and Otter. However, war was frequent. Either civil strife between individual chieftains, or from the continuous challenges of foreign raiders. Survival meant developing better strategies, weapons and tools than your adversary. Again the Blackdowns provided a ready resource for mankind, a metal harder than bronze, iron and the coal to smelt it!

There are several well preserved pits and slag heaps near Broadhembury to remind us that both local iron and coal played a very important part here on The Blackdowns. After the Roman invasion, little is known if the legions enjoyed the area. However, it must have been with some vigilance that a young soldier might make escort from Membury, over 'Those Black Hills' on a dark winters night en route to the Fosse Way at Axminster AD 150. Archeologicaly the Hills give us only a few hints of the Roman occupation, with ruins at Whitstaunton in the grounds of the Manor House. Neither, is there much evidence at the hill top forts to give us clues to any Roman inclination to hold the high ground of the Blackdowns, nor do we know how the indigenous people were treated. A race whom the Romans must have thought to be barbaric, independent and a troublesome populace to control at best. A reputation that was to last some time!

Human Patterns in a Living Landscape

Ancient and modern fields - Higher Luxton

Saxon fields near Stapley

The secret nature of the Blackdown Hills is hidden in the patterns made by the fields and hedgerows lining the valley floors and hillsides. Where each one is an individual signature of human endeavour and interaction with nature over the centuries. For when one looks carefully every field has a separate identity, each a compromise between nature and the expectations of men from the land at the time of enclosure.

The Saxon fields at the head of the Culm are a far cry from the vast expanses of modern day corn fields, with their grubbed out hedgerows on the high ground along the Yarty and in the U shaped river basins.

The very smallest and least regularly shaped fields may well pre-date Saxon times but there is a massive gap in our knowledge between the Romans leaving and those Normans arriving in 1066. Seafaring nations, the Vikings and the Danes raided the area regularly.

A great battle took place near Axminster with King Athelstan King of 'All England', seemingly defeating a great hoard of Danes in the mid 8th. century. The Normans established a few manors on the Hills but it was not until the early 13 th. century, that many of the valley bottoms were enclosed by groups of Cistercian Monks (a break away group from the Benedictine Order) who with the help of the High Sheriff of Devonshire, William Brewer, chose to settle the wilderness of the upper Madford River and build an Abbey just outside Dunkeswell.

The monks, a strict vegetarian order originating from Burgundy, were pivotal to the mediaeval changes occurring on the Blackdown landscape. The monks brought with them new farming methods. Wool was the wealth coinage of the time and sheep farming became the priority. The Abbey reclaimed large portions of valley land and established Grange farms over the Blackdown countryside. The estates became very rich over two short centuries, through trade, gifts and purchases of land. It was only with the dissolution of the monasteries in 1539, that the rich valley land fell into private ownership. Even so, there were great tracts of moor on the high plateaux remaining common land and unimproved until the beginning of the mid 18th. century.

Even then, the uplands were left as common land for those who were wily and strong enough to glean some form of subsistence from the harsh environment found there. It was not until The Parliamentary Enclosure Acts of the 19th. century that this heathland was developed into the larger fields, such as those to be found East of Churchinford and at Dunkeswell today.

High Banks and Homesteads

Another main feature of the Blackdowns is the wealth of high banked and hedged lanes, tracks and roads which take the unsuspecting traveller quite by surprise, when leaving the security of the flat tops of the plateaux. On descending into the valleys, one is confronted by the uncertain twists, turns and switch backs, which less than 60 years ago were the mud and cobble of the original cart tracks and pathways. Tarmac and concrete hasn't subdued the unruly patterns these lanes take through the hillsides of greensand, rock and clay. Like streams of water they seem to have meandered in their own way, almost as a natural discourse with nature.

The high banks either side of these narrow lanes, are virtual living historical monuments, many dating back to the 14 th. century, some far beyond into the prehistoric times. Devon and Somerset were the first counties where the open field system was subjected to mass enclosure. The boundaries of each were marked by deep trenches with the soil thrown up into mounds, creating the famous high Devonshire banks. These were then planted out with hawthorn, holly, beech and various other species of trees and shrubs to prevent stock from breaking out and straying onto neighbouring land.

Most of the villages, hamlets and outreaching farmsteads were probably settled by the middle of the 1300's here on the hills. Quaint homes of both rich and poor reveal themselves around almost every twist and turn of the valley lanes. Those to the West of the AONB are predominantly in the Devon longhouse or cottage style. The further East we travel the cob and thatch changes to flint, chert and ham stone with occasional soft blue lias, roofed with slates or tiles. Farmsteads on the whole remain complete, with barns, garden walls and outbuildings forming traditional 'U' shapes around a yard where stock could be easily corralled and sorted.

Warm work on a Winter's day for Father and son, 'laying in beech' on high banks near Dunkeswell. Saplings of beech and the bendy hazel make for the very best of natural stock fences.

Offcuts of mature trees or 'fallins' are put to good use by local craftsmen. Mature Oaks, Ash and Beech are guarded well by the Blackdowners in protection of the landscape, despite the law allowing 5% to be cut per annum !

The Power of Water

Water in almost all of it's collective forms can be found in the Blackdowns to form an abundance of rivers, streams, ponds, lakes and reservoirs. It has shaped and carved the landscape into deep clefted valleys out of what once was an almost completely flat, upthrust ancient sea bed.

The 12 kilometres of Northern escarpment on the Blackdown Plain overlooking the Tone Vale, is just what it appears to be, a 200 meter high cliff face! Limestone, the compounded deposit from the remains of millions of sea creatures litter the arable fields overlooking the town of Chard and hedges are underpinned with walls of the same white material. The three great valleys of the Culm, Otter and Yarty have been etched out of the greensand. Drainage through the material is good but water builds up pressure when it meets the hard non-permeable rock and clays, which make up the lower lias and rheatic beds, forcing springs to exit under pressure along the valley sides. At Five Head River on the North Eastern escarpment natural springs of water can be found forcing themselves through the igneous rock. Others just push up to form mires and bog amongst the forestry.

Photo Cathy Drury

Gay, chortling streams try to dive straight down hillsides creating miniature gorges, only to broaden their voices in joyful social occasion as they join each other to become small riverlettes.

As the streams deepen and widen into rivers proper they loose the impatience of youth. As we do in middle age, they seem to find control and purposefully meander, with slow dignified and python like patterns through the U shaped, widening valley floors. With each cubic centimetre of water goes another tiny fragment of the ancient sea bed back from whence it came, to salt water. It is this interaction between water and the very special geology to be found on the Blackdowns, which has made the unique landscape, as this is the only greensand plain in this country. The Culm River joins the Exe just East of Exeter, the Yarty to the Axe below Axminster and the Otter to it's own estuary and the English Channel at the seaside town of Budleigh Salterton.

TREES AND PLANT LIFE

The vegetation to be found on the Blackdowns Hills is as varied and colourful as the changing landscapes upon which it grows. The wealth of indigenous plants and trees indicate the results of more traditional farming methods which have survived here, in comparison to the more vitriolic methodologies of most lowland farms. Despite this, much heathland has been lost to the improvement for pasture land. Intensive crop growing and large conglomerate farming is not so active at the head of the valleys but further down the river valleys and on the high flat plains intensive arable cultivation takes place on the larger scale fields. On the whole most farms are worked in comparatively traditional styles. Medium sized milking herds, fine store cattle, sheep and free range pigs can be seen scattered in the fields. Although pigs kept on steep land can erode the soil to cause irreparable damage. Siliage and meadow hay provide feed in winter.

Some exotic crops are grown, like oil seed rape, linseed, and maize silage. Towards Sheldon, vegetables add to the profusion of colourful field patterns. Market gardens and the apple Orchards at Culm Pine Barton make for fantastic blossoms in the Springtime .

'Sympathetic Farming' has preserved a profusion of wild flower species to be found on the tops of hedgerows, in woodland, along lanes and in unpolluted meadowland. Swathes of Bluebells cut across the landscapes in Springtime in quantities to take your breath away and herb meadows full of Vernal, Knapweed and Crested Dogs Tail Grass turn yellow and pink in high Summer, with profusions of Buttercups, Dandelions and Red Campions in the fields to complement the highly coloured hedgerows. Rare Orchids and Sundews are to be found on the heathland, along with Ling, Toadflax, Western Gorse and Bell Heathers. Swathes of Foxgloves and Crimson Willow Herb appear as a million red headed spectators to the adventurer travelling between the high banked lanes, at the height of Summer. Violets, wild Strawberries and Primroses cover the banks of the wooded valley sides, to give way to Dog Roses, Ferns, Sloes, wartle and Blackberries towards Autumn. Horse and the smaller Field Mushrooms grow in meadows and fairy rings of both Red and White Clovers can be found by those who are pure in heart, or those who just happen to be walking past that way.

Marsh Marigolds and rare Bog Orchids can be found amongst the Purple Moorgrass tussocks. Bog Ashphodel, Culm Grass and Pond Weed thrive in the peaty bogs of Tricky Warren and Bull rushes with Fragrant Pink Orchids line the winding streams.

Magnificent towers of Beech trees play sentinel along many stretches of road, the best example of which is at Culmhead and into the valley of the Madford River near Fishponds. A wealth of deciduous trees grace the great forests of Neroche, Staple and Leigh Hill along the Northern Scarp and to the West those of Hembury and Sheldon. The ancient forests date back to at least the 16 th. century when records began. Ash, Oak, Mountain Ash, Holly, Beech, Field Maple, Elder, Willow and Birch are but a few of the indigenous large tree species to be found here.

There are no less than 646 hectacres of land containing sites of special scientific interest and there are 153 hectacres of Nature reserve, either managed by the Devon Wildlife Trust (DWT), or the Somerset Trust for Nature Conservation (STNC). Other areas like Castle Neroche, Otterford Lakes, Leigh Hill and Wellington Hill are managed by the Forestry Commission, South West Water, The Crown Estates, or the National Trust. There are however, many privately owned forest projects on the Blackdowns with a trend to growing trees only for profit. Most are planting coniferous varieties of quick growing, quick return, non indigenous pine species. Although colourful, these dark green lozenges on the landscape do not provide the abundant natural environment needed to support the great varieties of Wildlife indigenous to the Blackdowns. Nor do they have roots deep enough to keep soil from eroding and strip logging without leaving growth will also cause erosion of the delicate peaty soils and greensand.

BLACKDOWN BIRD LIFE

The Blackdown Hills provide a habitat for many British animal and bird life species! In addition, there are several rare butterflies and other insects seldom found elsewhere and both summer and winter bird visitors are attracted here from foreign shores.

The intrepid Buzzard can be spotted by the side of almost any road at any time on the high ground. Alongside them, occasional Sparrow Hawks, Kestrels and Peregrine Falcons eat at the high table of the food chain pecking order.

Rookeries decorate many older tree branches and clouds of these often misaligned and communal minded creatures gather in the meadows on a windy day, as might farmers at a county fair for the chance of gossip. The only obvious purpose for these birds to congregate, seemingly to have a good day out and catch a good few up-draughts.

The fortunate woodland walker might be honoured by the flying flash of colour from a Jay, or the tap, tap of a Green or Great spotted Woodpecker. Wood Warblers and Chiffcaffs fill your journey with woodland music and Blackbirds pipe 'pip pip' at your coming. In Springtime the hedgerows and meadows are filled with nesting Wren, Dunnock, Nuthatch, Titmouse, Pied, Grey and Yellow Wagtails, Gold Finch, Chaff and Bull Finch, Robin, Mistle and Song Thrush, to name only a few.

Meadow and Sky Lark song can still be heard high above a summer's cornfield a'top the Common land. Linnets, Yellow Hammers, Grasshoppers and Willow Warblers dart in and out of the yellow gorse and furze. Swifts, Swallows and House Martins make good the wealth of flying insect life. The heathlands are a special breeding area for the rare Nightjar and unimproved grasslands give opportunities for Snipe, Lapwings, Curlews and Reed Buntings to flourish. Special to the Blackdowns are the Owls, mainly Tawny. The smaller, foreign Little Owl might also be seen to visit now that the climate has become warmer. The Barn Owl, however, finds the high escarpments inhospitable and the valleys become ever more difficult for this beautiful creature as barns are converted to human habitation.

Worldy Cockbird survives on top the hedge!

Abundant streams and ponds attract a great variety of water loving birds. Herons can often be seen along the reaches of the Culm, Yarty and Otter Rivers. Coots and Moorhens can be found near the slower flowing streams, lakes and ponds. Wild Canada Geese are regular Spring visitors to several old quarries which have formed small lakes. Here they make their home until high summer to bring up their young. Mallard and Golden Pheasants are plentiful, having been introduced by game keepers for the winter's shooting season. You can spot the survivors with ease. The cock birds resplendent in Gold, violet and emerald plumage. The wisest birds have the longest tail feathers. By keeping to ground and fooling the oncoming beaters they have found a sure route to survival. Partridge, Snipe and Woodcock also make sport for the woodsman during the shooting season. The Common wood pigeon is exactly that here on the Blackdowns. It's soft mellow call harmonising with that of pairs of corn doves in a summertime dawning. Indeed! the Blackdowns do have a wealth of winged creatures who are a privilege to know and long may they be protected.

Fur, Feather and Game

The abundance and variety of bird life to be found on the Blackdown AONB indicates that there are still healthy eco systems to maintain them. The area makes for a rich habitat.

This is not to say there have not been disasters. Pollution from abattiors and farm slurry run off have taken their toll on river fish stocks. Rabbits, hare and badgers are always under culling threats from the Ministry of Agriculture. Fortunately nature has at least shown her resolve in providing rabbit families with a resistance to that dreadful man made disease, myxomatosis.

Otters can been seen once again along the banks of the rivers if you are very quiet. There is much evidence of well entrenched Badger sets on hillsides and in woodland. Weasels and their smaller counterparts the Red Coated Stoat scurry through forest floor vegetation. The Grey Squirrel has unfortunately conquered the indigenous Red. Hedgehogs, Wood Mice and very rare Dormice scurry unseen in the leafy dampness at the base of the high hedgerows to silently go about their business of foraging for slugs, worms and larvae.

Mr. Mole makes his a lifetime of similar pursuit, well hidden beneath our feet.

Grass snakes sun themselves in the flattened grass, or where sunshine falls through the leaf canopy to the forest floors.

On the high common land your feet may disturb the discrete adder to seek cover. So dense is the vegetation, that Slow Worms and Common Lizards go about their business hardly noticed by the comings and goings of walkers. Both Fallow and Roe Deer can be found on the Blackdowns. The Fallow begins its rut in October the Roe in July. Both give birth to their young fawns in June. If you find a fawn leave it well alone and walk away. It's mother will be in attendance nearby. Touch it and she will surely discard it!

The deer are managed by selective culling otherwise the health of the herds would deteriorate. They can increase in numbers at a rate of one third per annum. Outside of occasional road accidents these fey and gentle creatures have no natural predator, save that a lucky fox might chance across a weakly fawn.

Foxes are numerable in the valleys and on the escarpments with ample sustenance in the shape of rabbits, nesting birds, worms, larvae and the gamekeeper's pheasants. Mr. Reynard is at the top of the mammal food chain. Outside of the game keeper's rifle, natural causes and an occasional visit from the fox hounds, there is little to threaten this wily critter on the Blackdowns.

During the early nineties there were several reports of an animal roaming the Blackdowns which could easily box Mr. Reynard into a corner anytime! A Black Panther! I have heard of three accounts from good honest woods people of a cat like animal, that could be 9 ft. long from tip to 'tale' ! Snap a Photo and back off quietly if you chance a meeting. We are told it could take anything it likes.

Insect Life on The Blackdowns

Like them or hate them, insects are an integral part of the food chain and are essential to the ecological character of the Blackdowns. Abundant water through a variety of habitats guarantees an amazing selection of these almost alien creatures. Broad leafed woodland, rotting vegetation, stagnant ponds, wet heathland, valley mires, bogs, marshes, herb rich meadows, acid heathland, streams, rivers and natural grasslands provide perfect breeding habitats for a great variety of insect species. Their numbers far too great to list here.

These insects are a staple diet to our summer feathered visitors. Likewise, those insects that fly at evening time are the sustenance of the Common and Grey Long Eared Bats to be found flitting in the dusk, alongside the architectural loving Seretones and Pipistrelles.

It would be easy to discriminate against the great ugly and crop damaging Leatherjackets (Crane Fly Larvae) and Wireworms (Click Beetle Larvae) when there are a profusion of graceful and kindly creatures like the May, Damsel and Dragon flies to be found hovering over water. Yet these human perceptions are not valid. All species, ugly to our eyes or not have a vital ecological role to play here. Longhorn beetles share the nutrients of fallen trees with Proturans, Crane Flies, Millipedes, Centipedes and a host of Spider species. Beech trees provide a special habitat for hibernating Ladybirds in vacated dry nuthatch holes. Wherever water seeps into a tree trunk provides a habitat for Mosquitoes and Drone Flies to breed and feed on the tiny Protozoans to be found there. All are food for something!

Beneath the leaf litter, Harvest and Wolf spiders hunt through last years leaves for Red Soil Mites, Bristletails and Springtail Insects. Despite considerable armour and a fearsome chemical armoury, Woodlice succumb in great numbers to Centipedes, Toads, and Shrews .

Weevils utilise the leafy canopy in great numbers for food, breeding places and shelter. Many varieties roll up inside a leaf to house themselves or leave their larvae within. Perhaps these creatures are the most prolific here, there is not a tree without a weevil species that has not adapted itself to the characteristics of its host.

The Woodland Violet is the essential life link for several types of Frittery Butterflies. The eggs hatch on the leaves some 12 days after laying and the caterpillars feed on the lush green leaves. After three moultings they hibernate in a rolled up leaf during the winter. On waking they eat and shed another skin, before they form a chrysalis for 14 days and pupate.

The Blackdowns are a notable habitat for the grassland loving Brown Hairstreak, Marbled White, Wood White and Dingy Skipper Butterflies.

The rare Marsh Frittery can be found in the Springline Mires. White Admirals, Comma, and Purple Emperor Butterflies thrive in good years when food, warmth and rainfall make breeding ideal.

Gaudy Cinnabar Moth Caterpillars decorate the stems of Ragwort and a host of woodland moths may cloud the night. Bumble Bees bumble, honey drones go to work. Blow flies feed off carrion, Hoverflies invade the nests of aphids, Wasps flock to the picnic jam and the occasional Airwolf Hornet startles the nervous walker to duck quick in the thick woodland!

Mysterious Fungi and Fauna

Some plant life on the Blackdowns should evoke a little caution in us all, especially when venturing into the countryside with young children and pets. Whilst berries and fungi are often attractive to look at and intriguing to touch, there are some plant forms to be found in the Blackdowns which may cause grief to the unwary.

Most dangerous of all is the innocent looking Deathcap Fungi. At between 5 and 10 centimetres in height it can vary from a off white green to a pale yellow cap. It matures into a flat light tan disk some 4 inches across. It is also easy to mistake for a mushroom, save it has a skin frill hanging down from the stem beneath the cap. This is serious death! A single nibble can kill and even the spores contain poison. It grows on woodland floors, meadows and even on your lawn and can be found through the summer and autumn months.

The Red Staining and Common White Inocybe and Yellow Staining Mushrooms can be found here also. We have never seen any Fly Agaric, those pretty red and white fungi so loved by fairy tale illustrators to sit their gnomes on. These are all very poisonous !

The purple Monks Hood plant can be found in shady places, the roots of which were used to tip poisoned arrows for hunting game. The beautiful Lily of the Valley and close relative, Soloman's Seal with its lush broad lily leaves and pretty white bell like flowers, contains poisons not unlike the digitalin found in Fox Gloves. Foxgloves too are deadly if eaten but provide miracles for medicine in the control of heart diseases, when taken in the correct dosage.

Yellow Columbines are easily mistaken for the common Buttercup and can be found on the lime rich meadows along with the infamous Deadly Nightshade berries to be found in the hedgerows.

- Just don't eat it , if you are unsure of what it is !

Deep within the bodies of dead trees and in the flesh of living ones, the mycelium of fungi, (a sort of cobweb stomach) suck at the nutrients in the wood. This, when ready, produces a fruit body on the exterior of the unfortunate host. The result, the strange and wonderful shapes we find attached to trees throughout broad leafed woodland. Most common on dead wood is the brown /black Banded Bracket Fungus. On living trees, perhaps the blue grey Oyster Mushroom. White Grey Stump Puffballs grow as huddled little characters on fallen trees trunks, with the larger Green variety often clinging onto the last remnants of sustenance on a leaf mould forest floor. As a child I remember jumping on them to witness the gassious explosions as the spores took to the air. I cannot recommend it now, as the wind conditions have to be right for the spore to find new hosts.

Perhaps the most mysterious plants to be found on the Blackdowns are the Ferns, Mosses and Lichens. Ancient plant life that has found no need to change for millions of years. Soil, water and tree types designate where a certain species can grow. Often what you see is the work of several 100's of years. "Leave them to grow where they be!"

Industries on the Blackdowns

"Although the Blackdown area is precious and unique, it is a real and living landscape, not a Picture".

This means that people with a variety of skills must be able to live and work here, even if this is an environmentally sensitive area. Rural poverty has historically been a part of life here in the past and it would be unthinkable if it were to continue in to the future. This could happen if the wrong picture was painted of the Blackdowns to others.

Through three centuries the Culm valley was at the hub of the woollen industry in the Westcountry. At the turn of the last century, silk hat and glove making plus wool weaving provided income for many families. This developed into the more commercial factories at Cold Harbour Mill, Uffculme, (Now a museum) the Silk Mill at Stapley and Axminster with its famous woollen carpet mill.

Agriculture and the services which support it have traditionally been the root industries here but are now in serious decline! Two other major Blackdown centres of employment have closed recently. The St. Ival butter product factory at Hemyock and the MOD Radio listening station at Culmhead. Nevertheless, new entrepeneurs have arrived and modern businesses grow up in the most surprising locations.

Most small farms only survive as mixed holdings, where country folk have diversified to other trades such as building, farm shops, B&B's, vehicle sales or ex farmers commute to other work off the hills part time, to maintain their life here. Others have not found it so easy to diversify and their skills will be lost to the countryside and those of their sons and daughters with them.

The Milk Factory at Hemyock

The Prings have been funeral directors and cabinet makers in the Culm Vale since the late 1800's. The tradition of passing businesses down from father to son, still exists here but changing times make it harder for the young people to stay.

Master Craftsman Ron Passmore

The village of Dunkeswell has become a sensitive environmental issue with the old airfield brown field site becoming home to several very diverse industries, giving good employment and wages to many in the area. However, there seems little determination from authorities to provide adequate roads for the traffic which services it. Dunkeswell has the deepest dive tank in the South of England, attracting film makers and people seeking specialist underwater training from all over the world. Wool weaving, auction houses, preserve packing and a host of small manufacturing companies make items as diverse as engine components, modular windows and all terrain vehicles. Leisure too has become an industry here, with a museum dedicated to its past and every conceivable form of flying sport available. The hills also support many cottage industries, pottery making, B&B, media authoring, video making, venison farming and crafts of all forms. A local appetite for good food and fine beer has maintained great pubs. These, along with farm houses and small hotels provide quality accommodations. For the independent traveller there are several holiday parks. Horse riding, game shooting and trout ponds provide sporting activities, and a wonderful local real ale is made at the Otter Brewery.

Travelling the Blackdowns

The opportunity for leisure activities on the Blackdowns never cease to amaze. From making death defying leaps parachuting out of aircraft at 10,000 feet to create the world record for the most parachutist in a stack to hacking a horse around one of the beautiful rides.

WALKING has been encouraged latterly with many rights of way being opened up with the help of farmers and the very active volunteers from the rambling associations. There are over 284 kilometres of footpaths, with additional Bridleways and Byways of some 69 kilometres. This does not include many of the delightful lanes and tracks, which if chosen carefully, are not so heavily used by traffic as to spoil a walk along them. 8 to 10 mile Circular walks are in print in an excellent book entitled, 'Walking the Blackdowns', by Michael G. Harding, (Halsgrove Publications). This publication on the other hand has examples of short pleasure walks, most of them circular and designed for the less vigorous with little adventures into the Blackdowns, that are accomplished easily from selected parking spots and pub car parks. Remember to have a drink or lunch at your chosen take off point!

CYCLING is by far the very best way to wheel around the Blackdowns. The level roads on top of the plateaux make for quite easy riding. Though those who venture into the valley floors need to be made of sterner stuff, with good strong legs in order to climb out of them. The five routes from which we explore the Hills described in the following pages, make ideal long circular tours by bicycle. There are also several cycling routes published through the Blackdown Hills Project and they are available at Tourist Information Offices, information points and Village Agencies.

TOURING BY CAR without good planning, is not an ideal way to explore the Blackdowns, as laybys and public car parking is minimal. Please do not block gateways and narrow lanes. Rather plan to lunch in a pub and ask the Landlord if it is all right to leave the car in the car park, whilst you explore the area. Dumpdon Hill Fort, Neroche and Otterford Lakes have parking. It is good common sense not to park up on grassy verges as this can cause damage or block those narrow lanes.

FLYING in nearly every form can be arranged from Dunkeswell Airfield and with Gliding from the Devon & Somerset Gliding Club at Sheldon. See page 18 for phone numbers.

HORSE RIDING is a delight on the Blackdowns. Hacking, quality instruction and livery can be found at : -

The Curland Equestrian Centre, Crosses Farm Curland - 01460 234234
Greenham Equestrian Centre, Ridge Frm, Wellington - 01823 673024
Heazle Riding Centre and Arena Clayhidon, Wellington - 01823 680280
Sheldon Equestrian Centre, Northcott Frm, Blackborough - 01823 681118
Livery can be found at Heazle - 01823 680280 : M&S Livery, Georges Farm, West Buckland - 01823 662180 : Netherclay Farm, Thurlbear - 01823 276313
Hilary's Horse Hotel, Buckland, St. Mary.
For an equine break - 01460 234460

There are some published rides available, developed by the Blackdown Hills Project and these are available at Tourist Information Offices and Agencies.

NOTE TO ALL VEHICLE DRIVERS.
PLEASE SLOW DOWN FOR HORSES
GIVE THEM ROOM & COURTESY.

Recreation on the Blackdowns

World War 2 provided the Blackdowns with a legacy of no less than 3 airfields. Smeatharpe is used by a hang glider club, a model aircraft club and is home to banger and stock car racing for the Westcountry. This land is mostly private and permission to use it must be granted from the farmers who own it. Dunkeswell remains open to the general public as a working airfield and it is from here that the majority of aviation sport on the Blackdowns takes place.

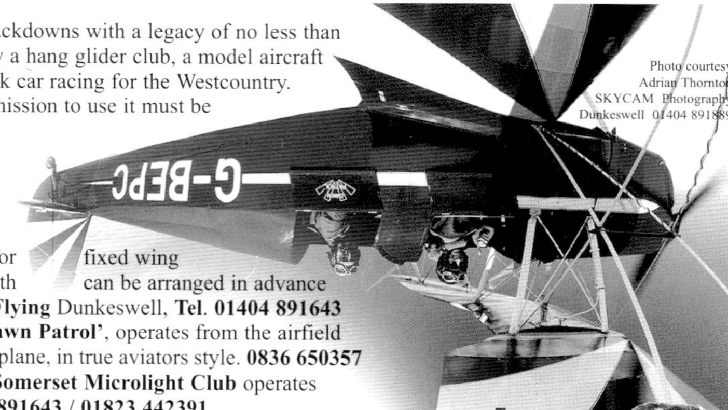

Photo courtesy Adrian Thornton SKYCAM Photography Dunkeswell 01404 891889

Lessons and flying excursions for fixed wing aircraft, mono and Tiger Moth can be arranged in advance at the **Devon School of Flying** Dunkeswell, **Tel. 01404 891643**
The very exciting **'Dawn Patrol'**, operates from the airfield with a fully acrobatic biplane, in true aviators style. **0836 650357**
For lighter aircraft, the **Somerset Microlight Club** operates from the Airfield - **01404 891643 / 01823 442391**

The Devon & Somerset Gliding Club operates from Hanger Farm Hill. You will be made very welcome. Tel. **01304 841386**
Go - Karting is found at the Dunkeswell Circuit in Summer at weekends.**01404 46384**
The South of England Rally School operates from Dunkeswell. **01404 891122**
Heazle Riding Centre and Indoor Arena. Model car racing & a variety of posted events **01823 680280**
The Dunkeswell Memorial Museum. Exhibitions in memory of the American FAW7. **01404 891943**

Golf can be found at the **OtterValley Golf Centre** (9 practice holes) **- 01404 861266**
Taunton & Pickeridge Golf Club (18 Holes par 69) **- 01823 421537**
Blackdown Hills Riding Club - 01823 601441
Hollies Trout Fishery - 01404 841 428

Those who wish only a proportion of their aerial time to be spent in an aircraft can take lessons and make regular parachute jumps with the **Devon & Somerset Parachute School. 01404 891690.**
Tethered and Free Hot Air Ballooning can be found with **Adventure Balloons on 01460 234597** & **Devon & Somerset Balloons on 01823 698757**

Cricket : Skittles : Walking etc.
Look to the Community Info **Pages 85 - 89**

VISITING THE AONB AT A GLANCE

NEIGHBOURING TOWNS TO THE AONB.

CHARD: Tourist Inf . Library . Museum . Hotels . Pubs . Hospital. Police. Train Station. . . . PAGE 21. ROUTE 1.

TAUNTON: Tourist Inf . Library . Museum . Hotels . Hospital . Police. Train Station . Market . Castle . PAGE 34. ROUTE 2.

WELLINGTON: Tourist Inf . Library . Museum . Hotels . Pubs . Police . . . PAGE 33. ROUTE 2.

CULLOMPTON: Pub. Police . DOC. PAGE 52. ROUTE 3.

HONITON: Tourist Inf . Library . Museum . Hotels . Pubs . Police. Train Station . . . . . PAGE 64. ROUTE 4.

AXMINSTER: Tourist Inf . Library . Museum . Hotels . Pubs . Hospital . Police . Train station . PAGE 74. ROUTE 5.

VILLAGES TO VISIT IN THE AONB

	PAGE	ROUTE
Awliscombe . P . Ch .	61	3.
Blackborough . P . Ch .	63	3.
Blagdon Hill . Tour Inf . PO . P . Pub . FW .CW . Gar.	37	2.
Beacon . SCW . FW . Hill Fort .	72	4.
Bolham Water .	68	4.
Broadhembury . P . Ch . PO . Pub . SCW . Hill Fort .	62	3.
Buckland St Mary . O. Ch . PO . Manor . SCW .	30, 31	1.
Birchwood . Chapel . SCW .	26	1.
Bishopswood . P . Pub . Chapel . SCW .	25	1.
Chardstock . P . Hotel . Pub . Manor . Ch. .	84	5.
Churchinford . P . Inn . Sp . PO . DOC . SW . SCW .	46, 69	2,4.
Clayhidon . P . Ch . Pub . FW .	42	2.
Corfe . P . Ch . Pub.	36	2.
Cotleigh . P. Ch .	80	5.
Coombe Raleigh . P . Ch . Chantry .	65	4.
Combe St. Nicholas. P. Ch. Sp. PO. Garage.	31	1
Culmstock . P . Ch . Inn . Pub. SP . FW .	54	3.
Dalwood . P . Ch . Pub . SCW . FW.	79	5.

	Page No.	Route. No.
Dunkeswell . P . Ch . Pub . Mus . Rest . Sp . PO . DOC. Flying . Garage .	59	3/4.
Hemyock . P . Pub . DOC . Castle . SCW .Gar .	57	3.
Howley . P . Pub . Hill Fort . Manor .	23	5.
Luppit . P . Pub . PO . FW .	66	4.
Marsh . P . Pub .	25	1.
Membury . P . Ch . Fort . Sp. PO . FW . SCW	76	5.
Monkton . P .Ch . Inn .	72	4,5.
Otterford . P. Ch . Nature Trail . FW . CSW .	29	1.3.
Pitminster . P . Pub . Ch . FW .	36	2.
Ullcombe . P . Med Village . CSW .	70	4.
Upottery . P . Ch . Inn .	71	4.
Uffculme . P . Ch . Inn . Pub . Mus . Sp. DOC . Gar .	53	3.
Rawridge . P . PO . Golf Centre .	71	4.
Rosemary Lane . P . Chapel . SCW .	42	2.
Sheldon . P . Ch . Brass Rubbing . SCW. Gliding .	63	3.
Shore Bottom . P . Hill fort . SCW .	80	5.
Smeatharpe . Airfield . Stock Car Racing .	68	4.
Staple Fitzpaine . P . Ch . Manor . Pub . SW .	51	2.
Stapley. SCW .	45	2.
Stockland . P . Ch . PO . Pub . SCW .	81	5.
Wambrook . P . Ch . Pub . SCW . FW .	83	5.
Whitestaunton . P . Ch . Manor . SCW.	22	2.
Yarcombe . P . Hotel . Ch . Pub . Rest .	24	5.

KEY

P - PARKING . Ch - CHURCH .
Sp - SHOP. PO - POST OFFICE.
Mus - Museum. Gdns - Gardens.
Gar - Garage : Rest - Restaurant .
SCW - Short Circular Walk .
FW - Featured Walk .
DOC - DOCTORS SURGERY .

FORTS AND WALKS

PUBS AND RESTAURANTS

PUBS AND RESTAURANTS	
Air Centre	Dunkeswell
Candlelight Inn	Bishopswood
Catherine Wheel	Hemyock
Culm Valley Inn	Culmstock
Cotley Inn	Wambrook
Culm Valley Inn	Culmstock
Eagle Tarvern	Buckland St. Mary, A 303
Flintlock	Marsh
Fishponds House	Dunkeswell
The George	Chardstock
The George	Uffculme
Green Dragon	Combe St. Nicholas
The Bunker Cafe	Dunkeswell
Greyhound	Staple Fitzpaine
Half Moon	Clayhidon
Holman Clavel	Staple Hill
Howley Tavern	Howley
Ilminster Stage	Culmstock
Kings Arms	Stockland
Leigh Hill Hotel	Rock
Lamb and Flag	Blagdon Hill
Longbridge Inn	Furley Nr. Membury
Luppit Inn	Luppit
Monkton Inn	Monkton
Merry Harriers	Forches Corner
Sidmouth Arms	Upottery
Queens Arms	Pitminster
The Ostler	Uffculme
Royal Oak	Dunkeswell
Tuckers Arms	Dalwood
White Lion	Blagdon Hill
White Hart	Corfe
York Inn	Churchinford
The Yarcombe Inn	Yarcombe

OTHER ATTRACTIONS

OTHER ATTRACTIONS	
Banger & Stock Car Racing.	Smeatharpe
Devon & Somerset Gliding Club.	Sheldon
Devon School of Flying.	Dunkeswell
Brass Rubbing.	Sheldon
Coldharbour Mill Museum .	Culmstock
Dawn Patrol.	Dunkeswell
Dunkeswell Parachuting Club.	Dunkeswell
Dunkeswell Karting Circuit.	Dunkeswell
Dunkeswell Memorial Museum.	Dunkeswell
Dunkeswell Flying Club.	Dunkeswell
Fern Animal Sanctuary.	Wambrook
Fishing Lakes Hollies Trout Frm .	Sheldon
Fishing Lakes Fishponds House.	Dunkeswell
Go Cart Racing .	Dunkeswell
Otter Valley Golf Centre .	Rawridge
Heazle Horse Riding Centre.	Clayhidon
Heazle Arena .	Clayhidon
Leigh Hill Hotel, Greendown.	Membury
Somerset Microlights .	Dunkeswell
Stockland May Fair .	Stockland
Membury Potter .	Membury
Taunton and Pickeridge Golf Club.	Corfe
Wolford Chapel .	Dunkeswell

CHARD is a noble valley town from which to start our first journey onto the Blackdowns. Links with the Blackdowns are indelibly etched in its history. Originally thought to be a Saxon settlement the town has a great vitality, with present day trade and industry reflecting a past importance for manufacturing textiles and farm machinery. Those travelling up the gradient of the High Street can't help notice the Town Hall, which doubles as a market, seemingly intent on devouring the pavement with its double portico and Tuscan columns. Little of the original town is left after the fire of 1577. There is, however, a group of Tudor houses which make up the Court House. The Grammar School dates back to 1583 and the Church of St. Mary the Virgin is worth a stop over having fine wagon roof and Jacobite dormer windows. One must presume the town had links to nearby Ford Abbey, founded in 1138 by Cistercian Monks. The townsfolk adopted its most famous son John Stringfellow who flew the first steam powered flying machine inside an old textile mill nearby. He conducted many other flying experiments from Bewley Down on the Blackdowns near Ferne.

The signs on entering Chard proudly boast of this feat in 1868 and his part in the aeronautical exhibition at Crystal Palace. There is a museum to his honour and the town's industrial heritage from the early Victorian era.

Our first journey into the Blackdowns starts from the town centre. Keeping the town hall on our left we travel the uphill stretch of the A303 past the round toll house and right to turn off right after some 4 miles to the village of Whitestaunton.

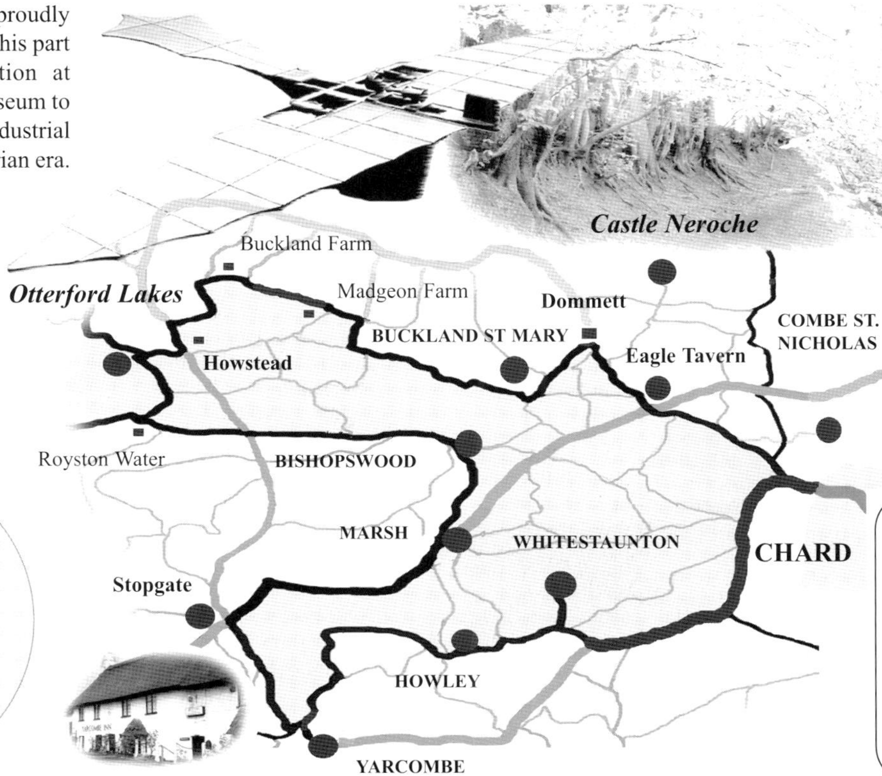

Chard Town Hall 1998

CIRCULAR ROUTE 1

The North Eastern Quarter From

CHARD

Whitestaunton a Capsule in Time

Just two miles beyond the landmark of the thatched toll house we look out for the right turn at the sign post off the A30 and travel towards the village of ***Whitestaunton.*** *Go straight over Whitestaunton Cross to drop quite steeply into the cluster of houses and farm buildings.*

Parking is difficult here without obstructing the working farm. The hamlet was once a Manorial Village of considerable agricultural importance. The Manor House, Church and a superb example of a fifteenth century farmhouse with extensive farm yard buildings are evidence of a once thriving agricultural community here.

Inside St. Andrews Church there are two 15th. century screens, a circular Norman font and 16th. century bench ends. It is worth walking around the grave yard if only to view the various buildings behind it, which seem to reflect in cob and stone, a time line of agricultural and social architecture. Set behind the churchyard is the grand architecture of The Manor House. Preserved within is the original 14th. century roof of beams on braces. A rare construction to have survived in this region. In addition there are fine Elizabethan Windows set by Thomas Brett to give the building an imposing but elegant exterior.

Joseph Greenfield the Vicar at **St Andrews** in King Charles 1st. time was seized and taken to the prison at Ilminster. His son the Vicar at Combe St. Nicholas was also arrested whilst attempting to deposit the ransom for his father. Both were removed to Taunton Castle. His son to lose his Parish to a Parliamentarian favourite, Joseph to die in London.

The Roman Villa built near St Agnes Well is on private land. The Well is a spring with ancient medicinal properties and it may have been a place of Druid worship in pre-Christian times. Excavations show the Villa to have a central court, frescoed walls, with a hypocaust to heat the house and pool. Perhaps the best way to view the Manor is to take the steep three mile circular walk which starts on the left, North of the village just past the Manor Gates.

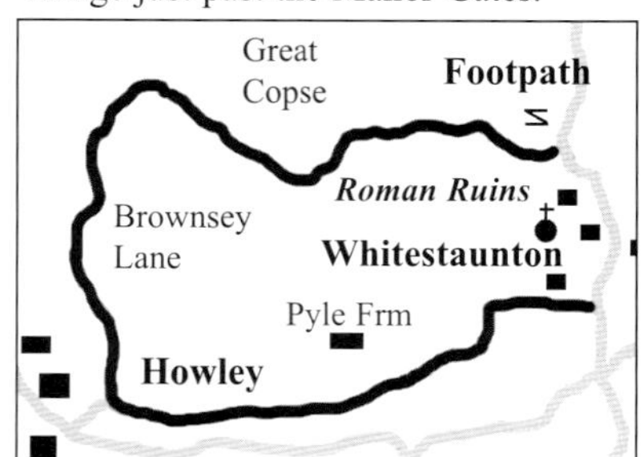

Howley the Yarty to Yarcombe

The 3.5 mile walk to Howley when taken at an easy pace will take around 3 hours, that is if you are not waylaid by a friendly local out in their garden or the excellent **Howley Tavern**. The same route may be taken in reverse from the Tavern say after a lunch, where you can take in the wonderful views of the upper Yarty from the garden.

From the Church at Whitestaunton you will find a stile on your left just over a 100 meters from the Manor house. This takes you over one of the small eastern tributaries of the River Yarty and across the northern face of Great Hill towards Great Coppice. The path takes you through the woodland and over a pair of farm tracks, one leading through Pyles Farm the other towards Laps Water Cottage. With Woodhays Farm high on the hill in front of us we cross the stream again to master the hard climb up to Brownsey Lane. After making a left at this lane it is all downhill from now into Howley Village. The path home can be found by a stile on the left just before you enter the cluster of homes, this will take you directly over the top of Great Hill giving you magnificent views over ***Whitestaunton*** *to eventually lead you to the South side of Manor Cottages and home.*

For the next part of our vehicular journey we need to return up the hill from Whitestaunton to the first crossway. We bear right on this lane and this will take us into the Village of **Howley**. **The Howley Tavern** offers a fine welcome, with good food and ale. It is from here that you can explore the village and the old **Hill Fort** behind it to the South. To find the fort just bear left out of the pub car park and take the first right up a narrow track. This has hard core until it reaches a cottage. After about 350 yards this will bring you to the base of the Iron age earthworks but with two Roman Villas nearby perhaps they were also used in that era also. To leave the village, turn right from the pub car park and follow the lane into the **Yarty Valley**. As you cross the river bridge stop to look at the fine **Sheafhayne Manor House** in front of you. This once belonged to King Harold 1st, Robert Earl of Lancaster and it still remains the property of the Drake Family ever since it was bought by Sir Frances in 1582.

The Manor House and Park land is extensive with the house mainly Elizabethan in structure but with modern additions in 1925. Interesting are the enclosed archways in the basement looking down into the river. Their construction possibly in anticipation of a fine landscaped garden. Our road route will take us past **Sheafhayne Manor** and lead us along a winding, pleasant high banked lane into **Yarcombe Village** on the A30. This was once spelt **'Yartecombe'**. Speculation arises over which present day farm was the original Doomsday Manor House of Yarcombe. Best indications suggest Dennington Farm. The village is steeped in history most of which originates around the Drake family and earlier as a place of rest and sanctity for those travelling between the Abbeys of the Westcountry.

Sheafhayne Manor

YARCOMBE and THE YARTY

There is a fine 5 mile walk from **Yarcombe Village** two miles of which are alongside the river Yarty at its finest and most picturesque stretch. *Just below the lovely thatched* ***Yarcombe Inn*** *on the opposite side of the A30 you will find a lane to take you deep down into the valley. After a quarter of a mile look out for a stile on your left heading across the fields to Chaffhay farm. Take yourselves though the farmyard and bear left onto the lane. A Ford is then directly in front of you. On the left you will find the route into the river meadows. Be careful if you have dogs with you and keep them on the lead as there are often sheep and cattle in the fields. As always have regard for the privacy of the residents. Cross the A30 and over the wooden bridge to walk the river and climb across the hillside up to the village of Howley passing just below the earthworks of the old Iron Age fort. The walk from here is confined to the quiet country lane past* ***Sheafhayne Manor*** *as you turn left out of the village over Howley Bridge.* From here on the lane undulates with the rolling countryside past several small farmsteads to finally focus on the 14th. Century Church Tower at Yarcombe.

The thatched and cob Yarcombe Inn, at one time called the Angel Inn, was thought to have provided lodgings for visiting monks from **Otterton Priory** and was a well known resting place for those on pilgrimage. It has a fine restaurant and real ale. The **Belfrey Hotel** opposite offers high quality food and country cottage accommodation.

The Breeches Bible found in the Church of St. John the Baptist is quite exquisite when compared with the computerised design of this page. Many must have been the hours spent lovingly producing it.

The Church of St John the Baptist at Yarcombe is deeply connected to the **Drake** Family. In the tiled floor are the Armourial Bearings granted to **Sir Frances** by **Queen Elizabeth 1st.** and there are linen fold panels on the pulpit from Buckfast Abbey given by Lady Drake. In 1599 a copy of the **Geneva Bible** (A Breeches Bible) was given by the Culverwell Family. The first known vicar was Robert de Chumleigh in 1315. Pig and terrier racing, as well as barrel rolling and metal ball throwing are village traditions. For several years The East Devon Sheep Dog Trails have been held here in July.

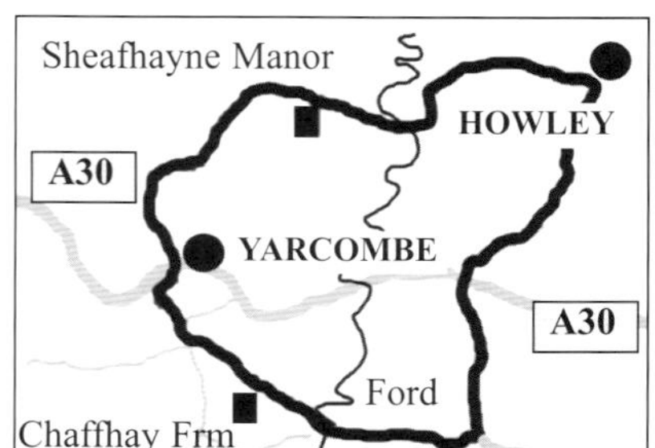

STOPGATE, MARSH AND TO BISHOPSWOOD

In order to leave Yarcombe on wheels we join the A30 and turn right up the hill. After 200 meters we take another right along the lane posted to Taunton. This brings us to the crossroads with the busy A303 at ***Stopgate.*** *In high season this can be a hazardous crossing and locals turn left towards Exeter, indicate and then turn right into the* ***Stopgate Service Station***. The shop offers a wide range of newspapers and various road side merchandise. Today there is no evidence left of the toll booth that once stood at the four cross way. A strategic point of control for traffic at this major crossway on the hills for centuries.

We go East for 1 mile to turn off left at the Village of ***Marsh.***

Marsh is an example of a linear village who's fortunes have grown and shrunk with the fickle needs and changes of transport.

When looking along the double row of homes down into the village on a still, frosty, winter's morning, it is not hard to imagine the many fingers of smoke that would have risen from the day's first stokings of forge and kitchen fires, as each household readied itself to service the needs of the busy horse drawn traffic travelling between the Westcountry and the East. From the turn of this century the horse drawn tradition of 100 years slowly changed to servicing the petrol driven traveller. The main road has since moved and the once busy street is now annexed by a by-pass for the A303, the hamlet to become an altogether more tranquil place. Yet, the Blackdown people are versatile to change and adapt well to work with the times. The once busy wayside garage now specialises in selling and servicing commercial vehicles, the cottages making ideal homes between Chard and Honiton.

A single pub out of the one time many, survives today with an excellent restaurant.

'The Flintlock', dates back to around 1745.

It is not only the name but the atmosphere which leads me to believe this pub may well have had a highway man or two at it's customer base in the not too distant past. Even, perhaps a barrel or two of smuggled brandy from the coast well hidden from the Revenue men.

The Route from Marsh to ***Bishopswood*** *takes us down a delightful and narrow winding lane past Elscombe and Foxenhole Farms.*

We can find this lane just behind the village by turning up by the telephone box and taking the 1st right. We have seen several deer on this road seemingly trapped by the high banks either side.

After a very long mile of twists and turns we come to ***Bishopswood.***

Here a mixture of old and new architecture greets the visitor. A superb modern Village Hall contrasts with the ancient flint walls of Otterford Mill. The village of **Bishopswood** despite its name has no Church. Instead there was a Chapel built in 1874. The mission hall was made up out of a pub, a cobblers shop and a dwelling house. A very active ministry survives today. The lane out to our right of the village leads onto the A303 and Toll Bar Cottage. *Our route now takes us to our left to travel east up the long hill to the high scarp road between Stopgate and Taunton.*

THE UPPER YARTY WALKS

When first entering Bishopswood, you are greeted by the **Candlelight Inn.** Originally the New Inn, this is an excellent base from which to explore the upper Yarty Valley.

Inns and Pubs were and still are the centre of Blackdown life. It was said that every second house on the Blackdowns was a drinking house, and booze smuggling from the South Coast was rife. This probably had some goodly effect on the character of Blackdown people and their ability to hold liquor and keep wit at the same time .

Not so for one farmer Caunter, who's horse by habit would regularly deposit its master at what was then the New Inn at Bishopswood for a night cap. This after a hard day at Buckland St. Mary market. On arrival he was often too far gone to climb out of his cart but not so far into his cups as not to be able to demand of the landlord to bring him some more of the brandy to which he had grown so partial.

T'is said, unless Mis'er Caunter got his night cap the horse would not move another step and would whinny all night like a chained dog who's heard the fox in with the chickens!

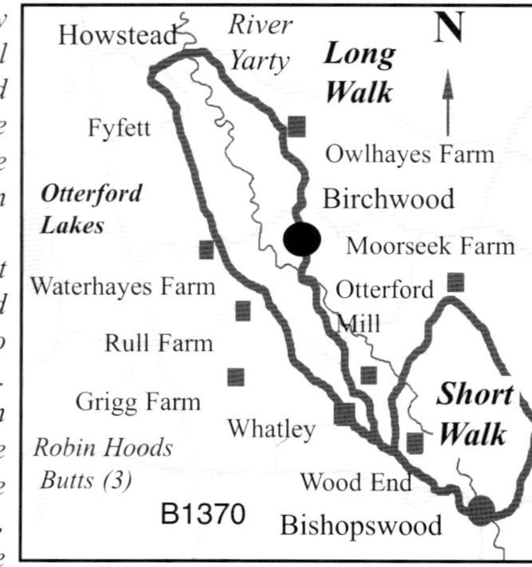

- Of course the brandy would do the trick and all three, horse, cart and Mis'er still in it were often seen parked outside 'ees home house kitchen door, come the sunrise.

The lads thought that it wasn't right one cold night for the Old 'Oss to be kept out of the stable. So they lifted down Mis'er - took the horse out of the shafts, took the wheels off the cart, heaved it through the kitchen door on its side and reassembled it inside. They put the horse back in the shafts, rearranged Mis'er back on top the cart - stoked up the fire in the kitchen, shut the door and left him to it.

To known knowledge it wasn't a cure for the old man's drinking but it does make you feel like you would like to have been there to share the moment, if not to stoke the fire!

There are several farmhouses with very wide doorways on our long walk, we might wonder which one might have been 'Old Mis'er Caunter's 'Ouse.

THE SHORT Walk 1 hr. From behind the pub, follow the yellow arrow over a footbridge. Go through the gate into the field opposite. This takes you up the valley to a track. Bear left across the hillside towards Moorseek Farm. With the farm above you, the path takes you down behind Mageon Wood House and back over the Yarty to meet the lane. Turn left back into Bishops Wood Village, just above Wood End.

ROBIN HOODS BUTTS & THE LEGEND OF GORM

THE LONGER WALK. 3.5 hrs. *Leave the Candlelight car park and turn right up through the village to turn right as the road divides. Just past the Village Hall you will find a footpath on your right. Keep left and this short cut will lead you to* ***Whatley****. The lane passes* ***Otterford Mill****. From there it is a good climb to the lane at* ***Rull Farm****. On your right is the public pathway through an iron gate to a series of stiles at* ***Waterhayes*** *Farm and* ***Fyfett****. This gate was blocked last year but remember it is your right of way! Farmers must be encouraged to include walkers and non have the right to flaunt the law! Bear right at the last lane to take you across the Yarty at Howstead and up the hill to a footpath right which leads across the steep fields, through* ***Owlhaye****s Farm to* ***Birchwood****. Here is found a delightful walled Church amongst deciduous trees where services are still held by candlelight. At the Crossroad turn right and then bear 1st left down Blind Lane keeping left to* ***Otterford Mill*** *and back into* ***Whatley*** *Hamlet and home.*

To continue on our wheeled journey, bare right out of the **Candlelight Inn** car park towards the B1370 Honiton to Taunton road and the top of Brown Down. Take a right! On your left hand side in a field you will find two of the tumuli called **Robin Hoods Butts**. Travel along the B1370 for a third of a mile and take the next left down a narrow forested lane to bear the next right to **Otterford Lakes**. Nearby was an old chapel used as a cafe in WW2, where on Sundays refreshments were given free to the Servicemen from the three Blackdown airfields.

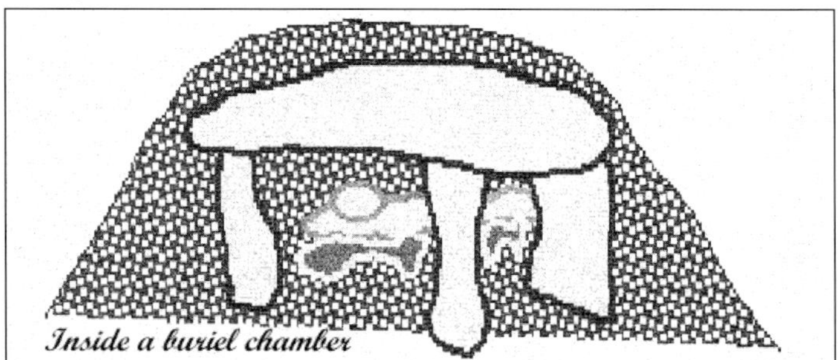

Inside a buriel chamber

A solitary horse mourns on top Robin Hoods Butt

It is plausible that ***Robin Hood*** *may well have passed this way to practice the longbow at the mounds. More likely however, is the legend of the two giants who fought here in stone age times. The least strongest* ***(Hengis)*** *stood on the higher ground, the other* ***(Gorm)*** *two miles distant at* ***Fyfett*** *farm. Both parties exchanged two massive salvos of dirt and rock grubbed from the ground. Both missed! Gorm's salvo created the tumuli at School Farm the poor chap unable to judge the strong Southerly wind. Next Hengis suffered from a severe hook and then a slice; his shots to go only a hundred yards either side of him. Both Giants decided to use even larger handfuls for accuracy. The fifth shot from the terrible Gorm went very wide nearly hitting Churchinford just above* ***Martins*** *Farm. The sixth shot from Hengis to strike the Northern giant soundly between the eyes. Blindly he staggered three paces to Bishopswood and then died to create the long barrow recorded there.* An artifact which unfortunately was put to the plough long ago. At Royston lane you can still see the clumps of hair torn out from his scalp. Or is it sedge grass blowing in the wind as it clings to the green woody bank at Royston Water?

TO OTTERFORD LAKES

The journey to **Otterford Lakes** is a short one by taking a left off the B1370 towards Royston Water to leave the central pair of **Robin Hoods Butts** on your left. Follow this lane down towards the River Otter until you come to the first turning right. This straight flat, narrow lane takes you through commercial forest for a third of a mile. Keep straight on at the 'T' and some 200 yards further along on the left you will find the small car park servicing Otterford Lakes.

The little pathway near the fishing hut takes you down onto the main track. This leads you down to the North lake and its formal bridge over a water cascade. Watch out for athletic fly casting, the fishermen cannot see you walking up behind them. The lakes are full of Brown trout for fly fishing only. A daily permit can be purchased at the hut but remember you must also own a trout fishing license.

What you see at Otterford are the remnants of a dream garden. There were once five lakes in an estate of 150 acres, at the centre of which was a six turreted House in Tudor style with four cottages and a lodge.

Photo Cathy Drury

The house was built by a Taunton surgeon, **William Bleadon** in 1841. The estate passed on to **Sir John Mellor** the deputy Lieutenant for Somerset. In 1894 the estate was sold to **Robert Lewis Lloyd** and leased out to the **Goschen** Family, one of whom became a MP and a Minister. No one is thought to have lived in the house after 1937 and around that time the estate as a home ceased to exist. A look around the ruins of the walled garden on the left just before the first fishing spot, will give you an idea as to the scale of the garden project. The woodland measures each season as carpets of white, yellow and blue.

In late winter the forest floors are end to end with snowdrops. The daffodils follow; changing to magnificent carpets of deep bluebells in early May. The Area is managed in partnerships between **Wessex Water**, **The Forestry Commission** and **Somerset Trust for Nature Conservation**. To discover this place, just walk the pathways and tracks. Otterford Lakes are a delight!

There is always some sense of mystery in a ruin especially when it was once someone's home. Otterford Lakes is one to explore at will. Touch the past in the flint stone garden walls, paths and laurel plantations. Hush!, is that the sound of coach wheels grinding on the gravel drive? Are those echoes of children's laughter past or happy dogs greeting their masters return across the red brick bridge? Otterford House in the 30's had squatters and a fire left it in a dilapidated state. The ruin was demolished when the Water Board took over ownership of the property for water catchment. It is a mystery there was no one willing to rebuild the home when it was such a beautiful setting. As this house died, seemingly also did that of a family line also. Become part of the intrigue and speculate as to what happened to all those who once lived and served here. For the memories of these Blackdown people are but all erased, save for the remnants of their love for gardening and the toil of their hands along the flint and chert stone walls.

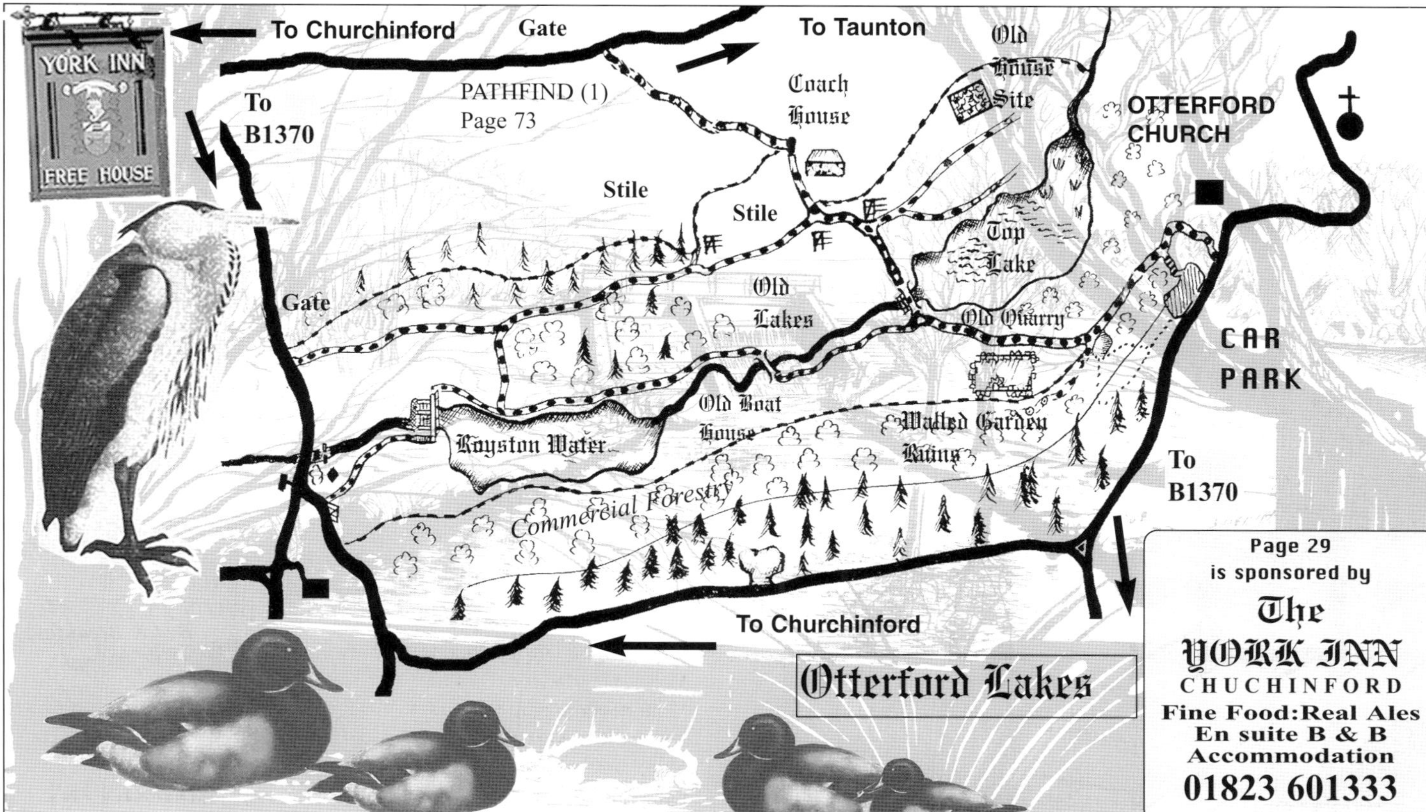

The Secret Heads of the Yarty

To leave the Otterford Lakes car park turn right to turn next left at the 'T' which leads you to the B1370. Turn left and go along this road until **School Farm**, where the northern most of **Robin Hoods Butts** lies under a clump of trees. Turn right off the main road onto the lane opposite. This takes you down through **Fyfett Farm** and into the first of the Yarty head spring bottoms. Here the shady lane partners the delightful windings of the stream at **Lower Howstead** before scuttling up the steep incline past **Westhay Farm**. Between the two farms the lane dips steeply towards the 2nd. head stream of the Yarty. The riverlet tumbles down the hillside into the deep clefted valley. The climb out again is very steep and brings you past **Buckland Farm**. From here on, the going is much easier. Take the second lane leading off to your right. This leads to a 'T' junction. Go left past **Madgeon Farm,** where the road will lead you to the 3rd. tributary of the Yarty at **Cross Hill Farm**.

" Each moment breathless, waiting for the first signs of snow melt.
Glistening before our eyes, heat and light as one.
Then bent boughs uncoil as snow dust fills the air and illusion takes for ever, as warm spring time takes hold." *MDB.*

Towering proudly on the hill in front of us is the Church of St. Mary's at Buckland St. Mary. Rebuilt in 1863 by the Reverend Lance the high tower is a land mark that can be seen for many miles. It is believed to be the third Church to be built on this site. The canopy inside is made of oak from the original Church. Alabaster and marble reredos memorialise the Reverend Lance. The screens between the chancel and transepts are built of Ham Hill stone, with marble columns and white lias capitals.

Inside there are pews for several hundred people suggesting that the populace of Buckland St. Mary was greater then, than that of today. **Katherine of Aragon** is supposed to have passed through the village to marry **Prince Arthur** and the Saxon name Bocland, suggests that the village was a seat for Thanes and Nobles. Also the nearby **Castle Neroche** and the association with the Norman **Count Robert de Mortain** must have made this village an important centre in the Blackdowns. During the 19th. century the village was prosperous supporting several ale and cider Houses. The Lamb and Flag Inn, now Flag House was an impressive hostelry. Today the village has a fine village hall and a well stocked Post Office Stores in service since 1874. **Mrs Butt** still works in the shop, athletically negotiating steps to the top shelves at over 80 years of age. Its like taking the same tonic yourself, as you shop here because of the friendly atmosphere generated by both her and her son William's love of village life.

The Route from Buckland St Mary to Chard

In addition to the Church, Edward John Lance built himself a new rectory with 9 bedrooms in the village. This was set in 37 acres of Glebe land. The hired help consisted of a butler, footman, coachman, parlour maid, gardeners and odd job men. Perhaps all this effort was in adoration of his wife who with a baby son died, perhaps in childbirth. There is a monument in the North wall of the Church with both mother and child ascending from the grave. He did however remarry.

St. Mary's Church Buckland St. Mary
The Cathedral of The Blackdowns !

Stories of village lads abound on the Blackdowns. Two brothers William and Joseph Dolland and one Robert Trenchard were brought to court for playing 'Fives' against Buckland St. Mary Church wall. It is unknown how it went with them but one must fear the worst, as they supposedly trod on the Vicarage cabbages whilst trying to make good their escape.

There is a short circular walk from here (2.5) miles, allowing you to walk alongside the stream which joins the Yarty at Bishopswood. Walk down past the post office some hundred yards and take the lane a little ways on your left. A few yards on your right is a track taking you down to the stream. Bear right along this stream and it will take you to behind the Candlelight Inn at Bishopswood, if you allow it to. However, if you take the right hand fork away from the stream for a half mile, this will take you up a steep climb to South and Cross Hill Farms. At Cross Hill Farm take a right turn on the road to bring you back to Buckland St Mary.

Combe St Nicholas 93 Photo Diana Griffith

We continue our journey towards Chard, leaving St. Mary's Church on your right to travel uphill for 1 mile to the 'T' junction at Keymer Cottage. Facing you is Dommet Moor. The bottom of woods have been a traditional Romany summering place over the centuries. A fact which Patricia Wendorf used well in her novel, 'Larksleeve'. A story based on the history of a house by that name and the travelling families who frequented the Blackdowns some 100 years ago. *Bear right on the escarpment road for a mile to the Eagle Tavern.* If you wish for some refreshment you will find a lane leading left behind the pub just before meeting the A303. *To continue our journey, go straight over the busy A303 past the* ***Street Ash Garden Centre*** *towards Combe St. Nicholas.* Combe is a delightful village well worth a detour if you have the time. It has a 14th. century Church, a post office and The Green Dragon Inn. *Staying on the main road will bring you to the toll house just above the town, from where we started our 1st. round robin route of discovery on the Blackdowns.*

MEMORIES

My first snow glistened in the still calm frosted air,
where small footfalls there were held in time for me to see
the proof of other creatures, who walked this earth with me.
Hand in hand with Aunty Silve, then lifted high above the drifts
Of Carlo and of Lucky, chasing rabbits long gone to ground.
The smell of fox, his tracks and then a deer!
the silence standing, craning still as if in a trance.
A Yelp! a breath of air, the doe is gone and in the clear,
to Tricky Warren or Adcombe Cover - to take the chance.
The dogs return and all a chatter,
"Nearly, nearly, nearly lucky", they seem to say.
Lucky's limping and all a bleeding through the snow cots in her coat.
My wellies too are full of snow and down my throat from falling over.
The sun goes out and the bitter cold is freezing,
I'm only four!
My tears mix in the snow with Lucky's bleeding.
No not for me but for the birth of memories.

MDB.

Do you have Photographs, local stories or poems that you would like to offer for inclusion in the next edition of the The Handbook and Guide to the Blackdowns, year 2002. If so we would love to hear from you.

Please send copies not originals with your address to Mike Drury-Beck, Litework Productions, 19 Fairfield Green, Churchinford, Somerset, TA3 7RR and we will try to include them.

WELLINGTON: A fort was supposed to have existed here in the 9th. century, during **King Alfred's** time. There is also evidence to suggest the town was a major centre in the Bronze Age. **The West Buckland Hoard**, mainly swords and amulets was found only two miles away. The infamous Judge Jeffreys made his mark here after the Monmouth rebellion, hanging three men behind the White Hart Inn and transporting many others to Australia. The town was very much non conformist and it was a Quaker family, the Weres, who introduced the weaving of serge to the area.. In 1799 Thomas Fox converted a flour mill on the River Tone into a cloth mill. A century later it produced one and a half million yards of khaki cloth for the army in 1915 for the Great War. Today the town manufactures woollens, mattresses, furniture and it is home to one of the countries leading chrysanthemum farms. The Parish Church of **St John the Baptist** houses the extravagant tomb of **Sir John Popham**, who during the later part of the16th. century seemed to own most of the Blackdowns. His body is not yet within the casement which contains only his wife.
The unpopular Lord's body was never found after drowning in a local pond. So glad were the people to be rid of him, he was cursed to remain in the waters with only one dispensation. That his ghost, if it chose to do so, could take one cocks stride toward his wife every Old Years Night. As his last resting place was from Beacon Lane Farm 2 miles distant, even some 400 years on, this fellow seemingly still has some way to go.

This sword set in the stone at Taunton Museum makes claim, amongst many other areas throughout the Country, that the Tone Valley was once a part of King Arthur's Kingdom.

From Wellington we head from the old A38, South up the escarpment towards the monument.
From Taunton we head towards Corfe from opposite the Sainsbury's Store in the town centre.

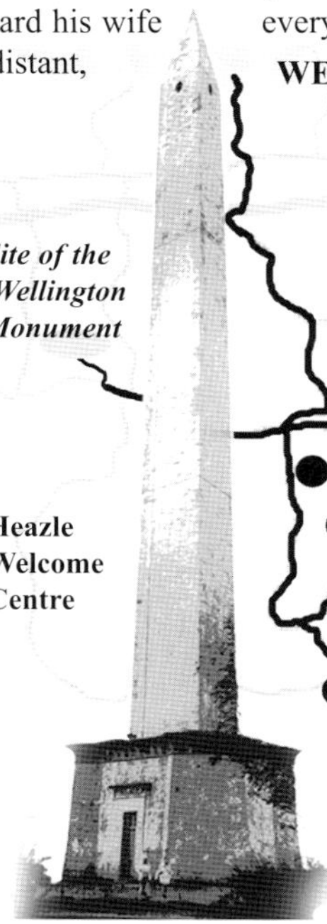

THE WELLINGTON MONUMENT

Circular ROUTE 2
The Northern Escarpments From Taunton & Wellington

Taunton Town

With the government expectations for house growth in Westcountry, Taunton and Wellington are likely to become the same town one day. Some 51,000 new houses are projected for Somerset by 2010. Taunton history, like that of Wellington has been intrinsically linked with the Blackdown Hills. An entry in the Anglo-Saxon Chronicles suggests the town was garrisoned by **King Ine** as a base for attacks to quell the British tribes holding out on the Blackdowns. With the coming of the Normans a large Keep was built at Taunton. The town was besieged and captured by the **Duke of York** in 1451 and less than fifty years later **Perkin Warbeck** and a rebellion of Cornishmen overran the town with the help of some of the locals. Perkin claimed to be a missing son of Henry 1V and marched some 8000 men towards London. They were put to rout by Lord Daubeney. Yet, the fact that Mr. Warbeck did not loose his head to Henry V11, might suggest that he did have some strong family connections. The town was a strategic stronghold for the Parliamentarians during the civil war with **Robert Blake** holding the castle until relieved by **Sir Thomas Fairfax.**

There are only few surviving buildings left in the town dating from before that era with many buildings burnt to the ground under a prolonged siege from the Royalist commander **Lord Goring**, who continuously attacked the town from his base in the Blackdown Hills. With the return of the Monarchy, Taunton lost its Charter and the Castle was demolished just in case it was used as a stronghold again.

Many good Blackdown men are said to have joined **Monmouth** when he proclaimed himself King of England at Taunton in 1685. The defeat at Sedgemoor proved ill for the people of Taunton. One Colonel Kirke dispatched some 150 of Monmouth's men by hanging, drawing and quartering them, with the help of his regiment of 'Lambs'. A little later, **Judge Jeffreys** condemned 508 prisoners to death and those who could not raise ransom to be transported, were hanged at Cornhill where the Market House stands today. The Castle Great Hall, once site of the infamous two day trial, now houses a fine museum collection of local archeological items dating back to prehistoric times.

The crown of Taunton must be the 15th. century **Church of St. Mary Magdalene** at the end of Hammett Street, although some might argue that title belongs to the **Somerset County Cricket Club**, during the Botham, Viv Richards era.

The large agricultural market behind Station road is amongst the biggest in the Westcountry, with a livestock market here since Saxon times. This traditional Saturday market still has the strong links with the Blackdown people and survives the many ravages of modernisation, with produce on sale alongside the auctioneers chant ringing out amongst the pens of livestock.

As we start our journey out of Taunton, away from the modern day hustle and bustle of this vigorous town towards **Corfe Village**, we might muse at how glad a farmer must have been to leave the hustle and bustle of such a foreign environment, as he returned up the steep escarpment to the peace and quiet of his home on the Blackdowns.

Villages on an Ancient Sea Shore

Once a long time ago, an ancient ocean covered the land where we pick up the Taunton to Honiton B1370 opposite the entrance to Sainsbury's Supermarket. **Taunton** is still only 20 meters above sea level at this spot. The ocean comes to within five miles of the city boundary when the Sedgemoor floods, with tide and rain up through Widness Rhyme, to lap the stone walls of Wrantage Mill.

We travel over the motorway to go due south past the **Taunton National Hunt** racecourse which holds some dozen meets on Thursday's through the season. An afternoon spent here is a splendid and friendly affair, the atmosphere around the paddock and stands is reminiscent of good old fashioned gatherings, where the aim is to have a good day what ever lady luck may have on offer. Top names come to ride here and Taunton is the home course of the famous trainer, Mr. Martin Pipe who's stables are on the Blackdown Hills, near Culmstock.

It is very easy to speed too fast through the village of Corfe. If you do, besides breaking the law, you will miss the 19th. century reproduction Norman Church of **St. Nicholas.**

The White Hart Inn (c.1751) appears on your right as you enter the village and it is at this wayside pub we turn right down the narrow lane towards the leaded Church Spire at **Pitminster**.
The White Stag is reputed to be a talisman for good fortune and a icon for good hunting. At least enabling a Landlord to draw a pub full of customers wishing to ward off bad omens with good spirit. Originally an Inn to Poundisford, the nearby hunting estate of the **Bishop of Winchester** and master of Taunton Castle. Today The White Hart prospers as a good food pub to the people of Corfe and Taunton.
Half a mile along the lane on our right, we can glimpse the parkland of **Poundisford** and the house built during the reign of Henry 8th.
Just above Corfe on a lane leading left off the B3170 is **Taunton & Pickeridge Golf Course**. Many of the fairway challenges can be attributed to an ocean of undulating hillocks left over from mining in the 19th century. Some are deep enough to fool the best of 3 woods and 5 irons. The club is open to visitors and runs a very successful youth programme. The fairways are spectacular and the club has come a long way since it was first kindled in the mind of the Vicar of St. Nicholas at Corfe and the Newton family of Barton Grange. The villages of Corfe, Blagdon Hill and Pitminster, despite a close proximity to each other, are quite different in character. Blagdon Hill and Corfe have grown in a linear direction . Pitminster in contrast has a distinct centre, emphasised by a cluster of homes around a fine Church and the one time mill, which now is a fine traditional pub, The Queens Arms.

Pitminster Village

Pitminster or 'Pipeminster' as it is referred to in the Doomsday Book was a 'Minster', or training centre for clergymen administrating the surrounding parishes. The ancient seabed on which the village stands beneath the northern Blackdown escarpment is very fertile and it is possible that Pitminster was a great agricultural estate well before the coming of the Normans. The present Church of **St. Marys and St. Andrews** is 13th. century, standing on the site of a former Saxon building. The leaded tower is spectacular and there is a spiral staircase to the left rood loft, dating back to 1400. The **Colles** family are much in evidence by the amount of family tombs present. That of John Colles represents the life and deaths of his family. Four daughters survived him, each shown bearing up their father's effigy on his tomb. Alongside, two baby boys lie at the head and feet of his wife Elizabeth, neither of them surviving the cradle. The font is 15th. century and is made out of stone from the quarries at Beer. The ring of eight bells can be heard a'top the Blackdowns, when the wind is in the north.

The Queens Arms hostelry is almost as old as the Church and the lower part of it was the village corn mill for many centuries.

Here is a particular favourite vision of a Somerset village. The Sherford Brook rises from Hawks Moor to ripple past both pub and Church. You might step from one to the other, without moving your transport at all, each sharing the others parking facilities at peak times.

The pub is homely inside, with fine ales and a good restaurant, yet it still retains a soft spot in it's heart for the locals. The most memorable of which is **Tommy Langdon** who's generosity of spirit and love of good drinking company has earned him a rightful place above the fire place, in a water colour portrait of him hay making. Perhaps Tommy encompasses the spirit of these gentle northern sloping hillsides and the people that have worked the land here for many centuries. In that hard work went hand in hand with hard living and the social life that was centred around the pub, skittles, the cricket team and the local dances. Embrace with him the wealth of country living on offer. Be quick ! Before all evidence of it becomes lost to changing ways.

*There is a 1st. class short circular walk (2 miles) from **The Queens Arms**. Take yourselves up through the Churchyard and bare right into the little country lane. This leads to your right. Follow this until the path cuts left to Woodram Farm. There is a path through the farmyard but it is generally very muddy and it is best to follow the path down into the Sherford valley over a footbridge that leads you onto Curdleigh lane. Bear right and this brings you to The Lamb and Flag Inn. Bare right down through Blagdon Hill Village past The White Lion. Just before the playing fields on your right near a bungalow, you will find a footpath that will take you home to Pitminster across the fields.*

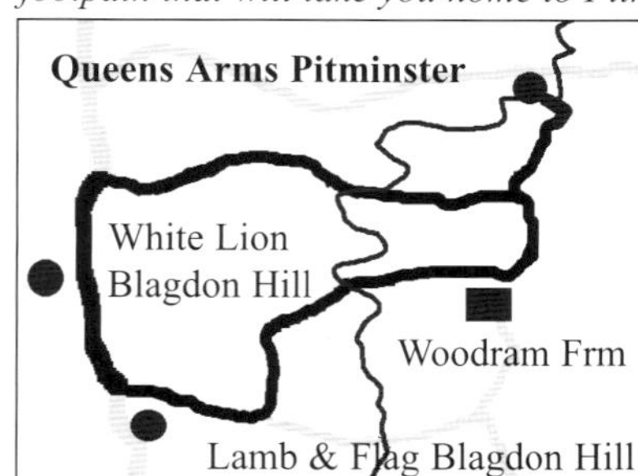

Blagdon Hill

We leave Pitminster with the **Queens Arms** *to our left.* A chest of French coins connected with the Monmouth campaign was found beneath the stairs of a local farmhouse here in 1815. *After a mile we arrive at the intersection opposite the playing fields at Blagdon Hill.* Home to not one but two Cricket Clubs, Sellicks Green and Pitminster. Blagdon Hill as a thriving village grew up around the transport travelling from Taunton over and to the Blackdowns. Sparks Garage is open for petrol six days a week and there is a Post Office and Shop, doubling as an Information Centre for the Blackdown Project. There are many cottages made from the local Blackdown flint and cherts, most notable of which is Blagdon House. As late as the 1930's, **The Govier's** string of donkeys might be seen back-packing the local stone from quarries on top of the escarpment, to repair the houses and farm buildings in the valley below.

Some say Blagdon Hill is Godless without a Church but in fact there is a Chapel at the 'T' junction to Angersleigh, run by the Datchet Evangelical Fellowship and there was a Church of England Mission Hall above the village green, now used as a workshop.

Blagdon Hill grew because of horse travel with a mill, forge, bakers shop, cobblers and two roadside public houses, both of which survive today. **The Lamb and Flag** (circa 1647) who's Tudor porch almost tips into the road, was attached to the coaching trade with stabling for hitching on extra horses to get the heavy vehicles up the steep hill.

The White Lion grew up around a similar business providing facilities for the heavy carting trade, serving only beer and cider until it became fully licensed in the nineteen fifties. The building and cottages date back to around 1605.

A nickname for Arthur Wellesley Duke of Wellington was **'The White Lion'** after Waterloo. Bric-a-brac of the time shows a lion rampant, with a right foot on a canon ball. It makes for some speculation that this pub was so named for the carters bringing the 1000s of tons of stone up the hill for the building of the Monument, over a 60 year period.

Both pubs are full of character and both serve a wide range of food and drink. Each has a skittle alley in the back, supported by local teams.

Blagdon Hill has its fairies according to **Bovet** the Victorian chronicler. He came across a Fair of Pixies when coming up over Blagdon hill. Perhaps he stayed at one of the two pubs to long. He saw what he thought to be a crowd at **Churchstanton Fair**. On nearing he became aware of a crowd pushing him. He bought a pewter mug and got pebbles for change. When he got home the mug turned to a puff ball but the pebbles turned to gold. Methinks Mr. Bovet liked a glass or two of cider or even something stronger, don't you?

Over the Hill and Far Away

There is an excellent long walk from Blagdon Hill (5 miles). This takes you through ancient forest and field from Curdleigh lane near the **Lamb and Flag**. After 100 meters turn right up the hill past Quarry House. Take the left fork into the field where the track will take you up the steep inclines of Priors Park wood. After a mile of hard climbing you will exit just behind Priors Park Farm near to the four cross way at the top of Blagdon Hill. You might turn left for some refreshment at The Holman Clavel or continue your walk by turning right, over the 4 cross way along the avenue of beeches that lead towards Wellington. After a 100 meters bare right, opposite Moor Cottage. This takes you down onto the old coaching road to exit onto a tarmac lane. Bare left and then a sharp right to find the short cut onto the new road. Look left on the steep switch back corner for the woodland pathway. With Luxhay Reservoir on the left, let the hillside take you back down into Blagdon Hill and right to exit just above **The White Lion.**

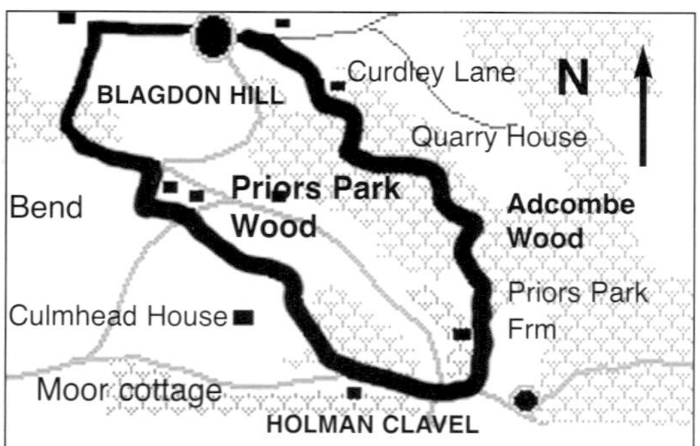

The Lamb and Flag Inn was a meeting place of **'The Parish Friendly Society'**, who organised care for the poor and sick as best they could before the reforms of the Welfare State!

On continuing our wheeled journey, the Blagdon Hill road is a daunting climb as it passes the War Memorial and attempts a 320 degree turn up a 20% gradient. It is said, that the coaching company sent it's most awkward and oldest horses to **The Lamb and Flag** as extra tugs for a cure or kill. The advent of the petrol engine, didn't deter the **Govier Family** from running a very successful transport business from the hill, up and until the 1990's.

At the turn of this century they owned a Lancaster steam wagon. A great lumbering beast which, would travel to London three days there, three days back delivering furniture for Chapmans of Taunton.

The steep fields just above the last cottage of Blagdon Hill were a favourite for tobogganing. In Winter there can be a distinct snow line across the hillside as warm air becomes inverted on the lea side.

We come to the crossroads at the top where the high flat plain of the Blackdowns begins. Our right turn takes us amongst the most magnificent stands of Beech trees each side of the road. Culmhead House is on the right and Widcombe Moor, the root waters for the River Culm, are on the left.

The Northern Scarpe and Forches Corner

Our journey West takes us through the lovely avenues of beech trees at Culmhead, past ***Burnworthy Manor,*** *now an Activity Centre. Just on the left nearby is a memorial bench set in a small coppice at the site where a Harrier Jump Jet crashed. The straight road brings us to* ***The Merry Harriers Inn*** *at the four cross way of Forches Corner.*

The Merry Harriers at Forches Corner

The public parking space opposite the pub is said to be the site of the hangmans gibbet, where several men from the Blackdowns who supported the Monmouth rebellion were hung. The corner became a favourite place for horses to become spooked and take the bit between their teeth, perhaps feeling the fear and/or guilt found to be in their drivers.

One poor farm worker on returning with a load of lime from Corfe saw not one but three figures in white, waving their arms at him. The horses bolted and he died within the year from the shock. However, fortune is a funny thing! *One 18th. century landlady, benefited greatly from the terrible noises she heard in her cellar. Summoning up courage with her locals, (all much too scared or drunk to assist her), she confronted the problem with bible in hand and prayer on lip as she went down into the depths of her cellar. "What's a doing in thar? ", she whispered as the candle flickered and started to die.*

Suddenly a voice answered her from behind a barrel of cider whispering, "Fear me not, you are a kind woman and do good deeds and I want to help you. Come tomorrow and underneath the stone, in the corner you will find something". The wily woman returned to her friends to tell them, "Sorry, it was just the cider working". The next day she pulled back the stone and behind it was a bag of money.

More than enough to keep her well to the end of her days!

Photo courtesy Monument Venison

The pub now provides a wealth of events and folk evenings as well as good food and a decent cellar to keep all its guests, tangible or transparent well satisfied.

From the car park opposite the Merry Harriers there is a well marked country trail down over the escarpment (2 miles) through a wood of hanging oaks. (Oaks growing on steep inclines).

We start off left from the small picnic area into Buckland wood to join the tarmac lane at Quants Farm and then back up the steep scarp lane.

We continue along the straight scarpe road for two miles, being careful not to miss the entrance on the right to the **National Trust** viewing and conservation site at **Quarts Moor.** To help you locate it, look out left for the sign to **Hill Farm Shop,** home of **Monument Venison.** Here you can buy farm fresh venison from naturally raised free ranged deer herds, beef from pedigree Aberdeen Angus and lamb from breeding sheep. The sausages and fat free pure meat is famous throughout the area and can be found on restaurant menus, at delicatessen and good butchers all around the West Country.

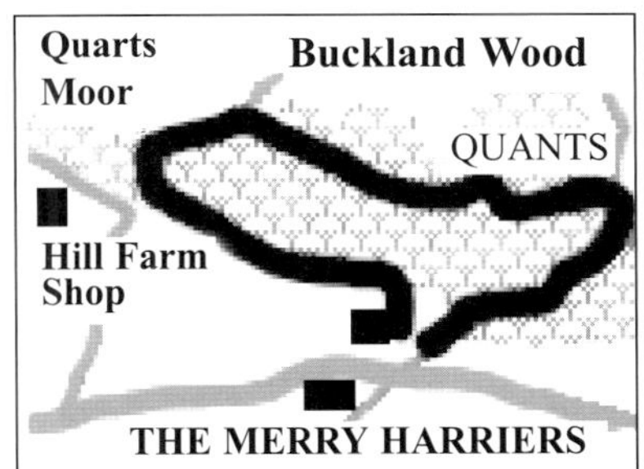

A Monument for A Duke

The National Trust have preserved several acres of the escarpment for future generations at **Quarts Moor.** The views out over the Tone Vale to Exmoor and the Quantocks are extraordinary. On the clearest of days you can just about make out the saddle between West Quantoxhead and Minehead. At **Quarts** there are several pathways leading through the dense brackens on the steep cliff face.
Fortunately for us this piece of Blackdown land remains as a nature reserve in the safe hands of the National Trust. One we can all share. You can walk through it, or just admire the beauty of this place from the small car park.
A middle aged Blackdown lady in the 1800's, who had never been off the hills in all her life, on seeing the panorama for the first time, remarked *'That she had never thought that the World could be so big! '.* She must have had a shock later on her journey, for she was on her way to seek a better life and emigrate to America!
*Our journey continues along the scarp road for less than a mile, to find a right turn into the hidden car park for **The Wellington Monument.*** This is situated near to the road but some 400 meters walk from the obelisk. For those with difficulty in walking it is possible to drive right up near to the monument, if the gates are not down.
The monument was erected by the people of Wellington and Somerset and it took 70 very uncertain years to construct it, with work being done intermittently. This perhaps, because of difficulties in finding funding and some would say the lack of will in a period of relative peace, to finish it.

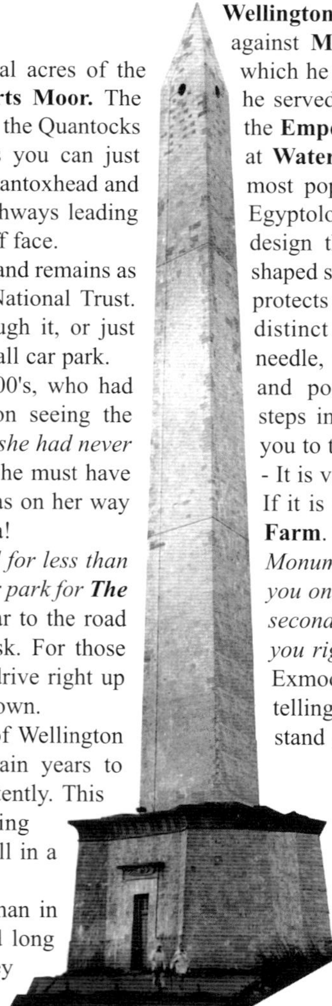

Sir Arthur Wellesley was born an Irishman in Dublin on April 29th 1769. His family had long held estates in Ireland, ever since a Wellesley rode as **Standard Bearer to Henry 2nd**.

Wellington had led the **73rd. Highland Regiment** against **Mahrettas** at the **Battle of Assey**, for which he received his knighthood. After that, he served in the **Peninsular Wars** against the **Emperor Bonaparte**. Victory in 1812 at **Waterloo** made Wellington, England's most popular General. The discovery of Egyptology seems to have influenced the design the monument's 170 ft. bayonet shaped structure. A cryptic winged device protects the entrance and the whole has a distinct resemblance to Cleopatra's needle, with its three sided topography and pointed proportions. 176 steeply steps in the circular stairwell, will take you to the observation platform.

- It is very dark in there !
If it is closed, the key is available from the Steward Farmer at **Monument Farm**. *There is a steep circular walk from just below the Northern end of the Monument but remember, what goes down must also come up. This brings you onto a lane at Leylands Farm. Bear right onto the lane and look for the second pathway to the right after passing the farm. Beacon lane will take you right back up to the monument.* Needless to say, the views out over to Exmoor and the Quantocks from here are outstanding. Nearby is a plaque telling you just what you can see on a clear fine day and several cannon stand guard over the great General's memory.

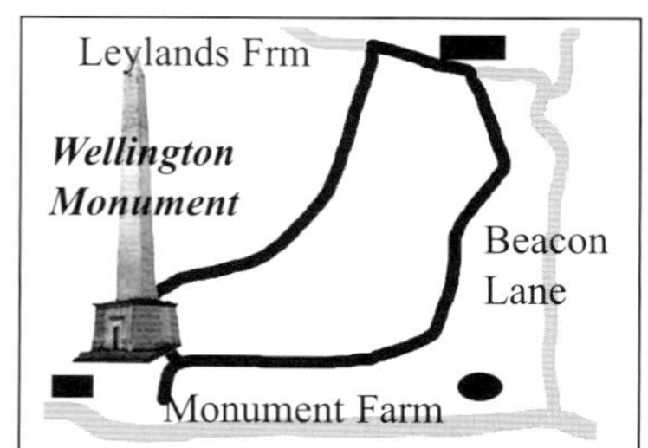

Simonsburrow and Heazle Arena & Stables

On leaving the obelisk to the Iron Duke we return east along our original path until we come back to the crossroads that lead to **Rosemary Lane** and **Hemyock.** The right turn points us towards the **Heazle Horse Riding stables** and **Blackdown Welcome Centre.**

At Heazle is found the widest variety of horse riding with tuition and horse care at all levels. An indoor arena and livery make this a premier equestrian centre on the Blackdowns.

The indoor Arena is ideal for holding all forms of events and it is fast becoming a centre for a wide range of activities. Prestige car shows, concerts and model car race meetings take place on the weekends.

From just behind Heazle farm there is a short circular walk across the fields to the East onto Red lane, (2 miles) which on bearing right leads down into the delightful hillside village of ***Clayhidon,*** *with its 15th. century Church and traditional Pub. After wetting your whistle, take the path running upwards beside the Church to lead directly up the hill to bring you back to Heazle. There is a good, 'There and back walk' starting at Jennings Farm which takes you right to Simonsburrow through a Nature Reserve (2 miles). This ends at the little chapel at Simonsburrow.* The hill in front of you is said to be where King Symond Lord of all Exmoor was interned in a Great Barrow.

Others say the barrow was the last resting place for Dumonian soldiers who perished at the hand of King Ina in 710 AD in a battle nearby. Could it be that both stories are the same but told from differing perspectives? **King Symond** (Sigemund) was not a local man and came into his kingdom by somewhat of an odyssey after arriving in England with a Danish raiding party. He was put overboard for causing a mutiny. Washed up on the shore he found himself in the cave of Old Mol the Overlord of all Exmoor, (Dumania - Devon) who's daughter he married. He then took the title for himself. He is said to have given the land for Wellington Parish Church to be built on but he is best known for his laws passed between A.D. 688 and 725.

Only the field names of Great and Little Burrow/Barrow Close remain as evidence today. A certain James Bale carted the great stones away from the barrows in the 1870's for building roads. It's a shame that the curse put on anyone who removed the stones was not effective early on during the excavations. We would dearly have liked to have seen the barrows today.

Clayhidon and Rosemary Lane

Our journey restarts by leaving Heazle past Jennings Farm down towards Rosemary Lane. The hill on our right is Clayhidon Turbary. and after a half mile if we take the first turning left up the hill, we come to the village of **Clayhidon**, or 'High Clay Down'.

Clayhidon's most famous resident was **Toni Sayers** the last and greatest of the bare-knuckle fighters and Champion of all England in 1857. Like the warriors of the Blackdown's past, this pugilist found the hills to be a convenient bolt hole! When the justices refused to give a license to hold a boxing match in one county, he was then very quickly able to re-arrange the competition elsewhere, with Clayhidon's geographical position at the centre of them.

The horrific gargoyle of a human soul being consumed by the devil at the top of the Church tower, represents an insight, into the desperate plight of the people who lived here prior to the coming of the **Blackdown Mission at Rosemary Lane**. The area had the reputation as a somewhat wild and nefarious place. Sheep stealing, smuggling and total poverty with it's attendant deprivation, were rife. The contrasts between the tranquil countryside and the immensity of human moral degradation confounded the evangelical preacher **George Brealey**, as he attempted to convert the wild nature of the Blackdowners in the mid 19th. century. A plaque set in the hedge near the signpost at Bollhayes Cross reinforces this.

"William Blackmore, Land Surveyor, Of Clayhidon Mills, Murdered on this spot, the 16th day of February 1853, by George Sparks of this Parish, who was executed at Exeter for his horrid crime".

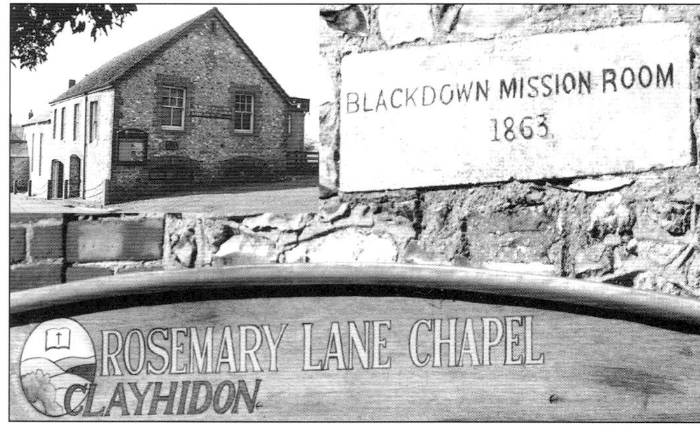

George Brealey was a man of great faith. Forsaking his stipend, he arranged for folk to immigrate to the New World away from the bitter poverty on the hills and the agricultural upheaval of early Victorian times. George brought with him not only the strongest faith in Christ but the practical humanitarian reforms needed to express it. A Christian faith with practical deed at its core working to ease the daily struggle for existence found here to make space in the human heart to accept Christ into their lives. Brealey 's Chapels can be found throughout the Hills. This is reflected these days on Sundays, where many are full of people both young and old still sharing this blend of communal wealth and Christian Faith. Brealey regularly practiced public baptisms in the cold peaty rivers on the Blackdowns.

A once transported sheep stealer recently returned from Australia, attracted an audience of 100's to witness his baptism in Christ. A much recorded event. For such was the miracle of it, that a man who had wronged so many, could receive redemption and become a Christian.

Into the Higher Culm Vale

Before the storm comes over the Higher Culm Valley

We retrace our journey from Clayhidon back into the hamlet of Rosemary Lane. This hillside cluster of homes are best discovered on foot. If the chapel is open, spare a moment in the humble sanctity it provides at the very heart of this place.

A circular walk (1 mile) from the Post Office Shop leads down the steep road past the Chapel. Just before the fork in the road a public footpath branches left. This takes you across the fields to Battle Street Lane, perhaps the very site of King Symond's demise at his bloody meeting with the Saxon King Ine. Bear right down the lane and you come across to Hidon Mill, where the murdered land surveyor Blackmoor once lived. Before crossing the Culm, take the right path to take you over the river bottoms and a ford, to bear right up Callers Lane and home.

Wildlife Reserve up the Higher Culm

To continue on our wheeled journey we go down the steep road through Rosemary Lane, to lead us across the Culm at Bridge House Bridge. Here we bear left along the Culm Valley Bottoms, past Lilycombe and onto Brimley Farm and straight over the cross roads keeping us to the valley bottoms past Lower Courtsmoor. We now turn right as the road forks and make the climb towards Churchstanton, past Court Farm.

The views of the Upper Culm valley are breathtaking and climbing up from the valley bottoms on either side is a landscape of miniature fields and insect and flower filled water meadows, that have hardly changed since Saxon times.

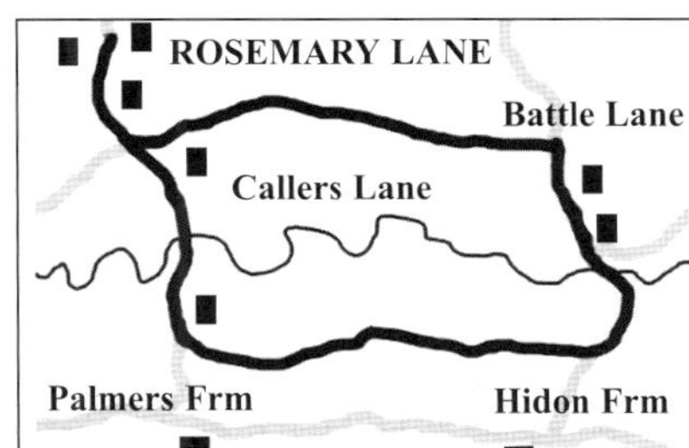

Churchstanton, Site of a Forgotten City?

Legend has it that there was a great City on the Blackdowns a thousand years before the time of Arthur Pendragon which survivied and prospered for some 500 years. It held a secret as old as Atlantis, where ordinary iron could be made to be harder than the hardest stone yet would not splinter. Sadly, the secret was given away by a love struck chieftain as part of the dowry for the hand of a beautiful Gaulish bride. One day her Kinsmen attacked with equal steel and the walls were breached and the people of the great Blackdown City were all killed or enslaved. The great city gates were taken back to Brussels as a token of victory. Only the great sword Excalibur was saved and several seemingly useless bronze cauldrons were hauled to the Welsh valleys by fanciful Druids. It is said that the Church at Churchstanton was built on the holy site for the city and that no-one dared to rebuild houses here ever again. It is also said, that the devil appears as a giant Calf in the fields opposite the Church and to touch any large stone at Churchstanton will bring ill luck. Strangers are supposed to be able to survive the place with a sound mind. That is - until after midnight.

As you come to the 'T' Junction at Churchstanton you are greeted by the picturesque 13th. century Church of **St Peter and St Paul.** One of the oldest known Blackdown trackways passes nearby on it's way from Honiton to Taunton. The Church has a square tower with a peel of six bells, a fine wagon roof and five naive arches. The window tracery is 15th. century but most of the original glass windows were destroyed by parliamentarian soldiers. There are 26 carved pew ends from the mediaeval period forming the front of the gallery. The oldest known artifact is the Norman font standing on marble pillars. The gallery is 19th. century and was designed for the female silk mill workers at **Stapley**. In the porch are the Parish stocks plus a 17th. century carved oak bier. The name Stanton probably meant stony ground. Ask any farmer here, he will agree with the analysis. The Saxon name 'Estandone' meaning Stony Town gives some small credence to the idea that a city existed here long ago.

*There is a 2 mile circular walk which takes you up to **Burnworthy Manor** and back down one of the prettiest lanes in the Blackdowns. Start at the Church and walk right down past the cottage on the corner. Just on the left, you will see the right of way. This leads you across the Culm river and into the woods behind Venn Farm. Be quiet here in Summer time there are pheasant breeding pens and duck on the ponds. On coming to Burnworthy Manor keep to your right and stay on the driveway. The area is used for character building, outward bound courses. Some hundred yards past the Manor House, the track leads off to your right and onto a leafy lane. Bear right and after a short mile, this will bring you back to the Church.*

Stapley to Churchinford

*To find **Stapley,** we must go up the hill from St Peters and St Pauls, Churchstanton and take the first right at the fork at Mermans Corner. If you are joined by a wisp of white mist in the daytime, or at night see the headless white horse ridden by its decapitated rider, it is quite normal here. Follow this lane along for a mile, then right again at the 'T' junction, down the hill to lead us into Stapley Village.*

Stapley has a Tudor Manor House where **Lady Jane Grey** is supposed to have stayed with her father Sir Thomas Grey Duke of Suffolk, the then Lord of Stapley Manor. There is an opportunity to stay in the village at the delightful **Pear Tree Cottage.**

The remains of the **Silk Mill** which used to employ 150 workers is down Factory Lane near the fast running River Culm. The village has no shop but a Primary School services the whole Parish of Churchstanton from here. Education takes place around a classic Victorian school building set in idyllic surroundings.

Stapley's most famous latterday son is one Mr. Ireland who was the first owner of a Char-a-banc on the Blackdowns, **'The Lady Betty'**. His famous cry to his son was to shout, **" Beetle Bert! "** and determine whether his trippers would get safely to their destination or not. At his father's command and not without some little desperation young Bert

Hidewood Ford

Mill House at Stapley

would leap out of the vehicle with mallet in hand (The beetle), as it ran away down the steep Blackdown inclines. When he was able to catch up with the careering bus, he would smash a wedge between the open wheel and brake block to bring the vehicle to a halt.

There is a Circular walk (4 long miles).Go down Mill Lane and up through the wood. With Paye Farm in front of you, turn right across the top of the plantation, to take you past Beerhill and Luddery Hill Farms and finally to take a right at the Farm atop Biscombe Hill. Then down into the Culm Valley, only to climb up the steep hillside past Grants Farm. Bear right onto the lane for a quarter of a mile and right at the signpost to Stapley, across the fields.

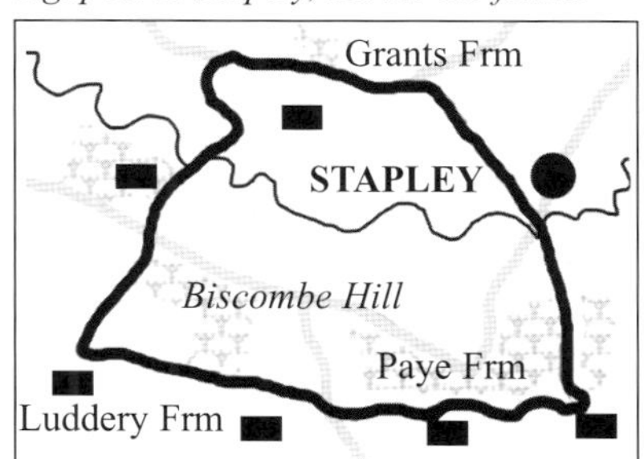

Churchinford a Living Village

We travel West from **Stapley**, leaving a 100 Saxon fields in as many acres to our right hand side. At the first turning left we go up Rainbow Lane to take another left onto Broad Street. One mile on we cross the Honiton / Culmhead Road into **Churchinford** at the 6 cross way.

Churchinford still has the real country village flavour, much of which can be blamed on the three main local services surviving through this century. **Foxwell's Bakery** is especially notable with bread still coming fresh out of the ovens every weekday morning. The 15th. century **York Inn** is a must for lunch or dinner, where the food on offer would be difficult to better in France. The friendly **Post Office,** where a "Good morning", makes you feel as wealthy as winning a jackpot on the lottery. There were once three working farms in the village but milk quotas have put an end to the daily sight of cows coming up through the centre. The amount of houses here has been extended by one 100% since the first bobby and his bicycle came here in 1919.

Churchinford 1997

Churchinford 1901 Note the 2 children outside the shop

However, the population has stayed very much the same with the decline in large families since those times, that and the fact most farms would have supported 3or 4 labourers and their families.

The village has the benefit of the brand new doctors surgery. **The Blackdown Practice** services an area of over 150 square miles. The red brick village hall is alive with Golden Age functions, WI, toddlers groups and other children's organisations. In late summer a beer festival is held under canvas raising money for musical instruments and resources for the local schools.

Culmhead and The Holman Clavel

Geographically **Churchinford** is arguably the most centralised village to the Blackdown AONB and we shall return here later to take a snapshot of some of the issues which effect village life at the end of this Millennium (Page 69).

We now head North towards Taunton from the six crossway to lead us past the forest of Radio masts at **The Culmhead Composite Signals Station**. Hidden deep within the secure complex you can still find the remains of the runways for the smallest of the three 2nd World War airfields on the Blackdowns. Fighter aircraft flew from here as cover for the bomber bases and civilian targets, with Hurricanes being flown by pilots of **The Polish Airforce**. There are several airfield buildings scattered around the area made out of blast proof concrete, which 40 years on are almost impossible to dismantle without specialist equipment. A certain chicken farmer wished to widen the door on one such building. Despite several days with a sledge hammer it still remains to this day, albeit with a few chips off the corners. The future of Culmhead is uncertain as the listening station is closing down.

Canny Blackdown Farmers put many WW 2 buildings to good use!

A whole book could be devoted to the goings on at **The Holman Clavel** on top of Blagdon Hill. We find it by turning right at the first set of crossroads after Culmhead. This is the pub at which **Chimney Charlie**, TV ghost and once defrocked monk takes his tipple. For he loves these earthly pleasures so much he still refuses to take the step towards eternity and remains the permanent ghostly caretaker. Landlords & ladies do well here if they are decent fun loving folk and believe he exists. The prerequisites for victualling success here are a tolerance for skittles being played in the middle of the night, the sound of crockery and glassware being broken and taking notice of Charlie if he shows disapproval of the timing for a function. You'll get the message well enough if he likes you or not. The tableware is likely to disappear and drinks too if you are of unfavourable disposition. The Holman Clavel is a lovely pub of traditional character. The Holly support for the massive Inglenook still exists.

The property is leased out by Otterford Parish Council, for the benefit of the Parish coffers. Just think every time you have a drink you help to diminish that scourge of all home owners: - in Otterford at least - Their Council Tax!

Walks through Rides over the Forests of Neroche

There are two great ways to discover the Northern face of The Blackdowns! The first is to walk the many pathways through the heavily wooded escarpment which lie between the **Holman Clavel** and **Castle Neroche.** The other is to fly over it on a quiet evening's air in a hot air balloon. On fine evenings you can spot the pilots and their guests in a basket, taking to the air from strategic points in the Tone Valley.

This must surely be the ultimate experience in viewing the fascinating, forested cliff face which used to be one of the greatest hunting forests in the South West.

Earthworks abound below you from **Culmhead** to **Castle Neroche**, perhaps one of the finest strategic holding points in the South West peninsular. Looking down on these hills supported by the colourful envelope of a balloon must surely emanate the surreal tranquillity, that lies below, with an integrity beyond that of any other.

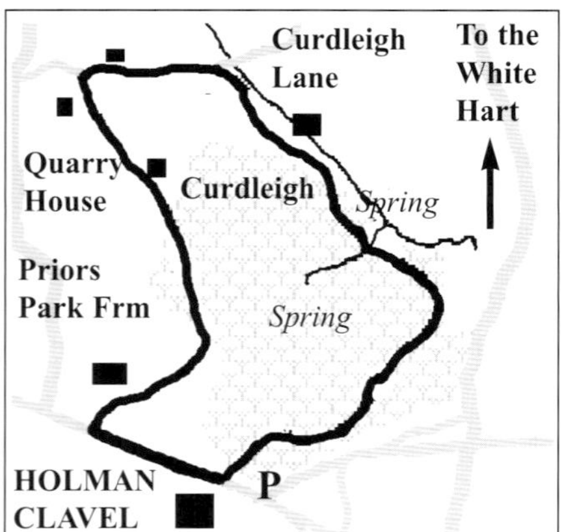

Walk No 1. *From the Holman Clavel turn left towards the four cross way. Just before the crossroads you will find a signpost on the right directing you past Priors Park Farm. This leads down a steep bridle way for a good mile to Quarry House and takes you into Quarry lane. This intersects with Curdleigh lane. Turn Right and keep right until you come to the valley bottom at Curdleigh. Go through the Iron gate and along the track that parallels the stream. Keep straight on through the wooden gate and up the long steepish climb, to the top of Hawks Moor (1 mile). Look out for the track leading right and this will bring you out below some iron age earthworks to exit at the Holman Clavel.* To find Staple Woods on our route we start off with the Holman Clavel on your right, to take a left at the 1st. fork. Stay right! Go over the cross road towards Chard and The Eagle Tavern and you will find the entrance to Staple Woods on your right, after a half mile.

Walk No2: *From the Gateway at Staple Woods, the walk takes you on the right hand path through Mount Fancy Farm to bear left below the farm onto Underhill Lane. Bear left uphill and take the track to your left through the conifers and then home.*

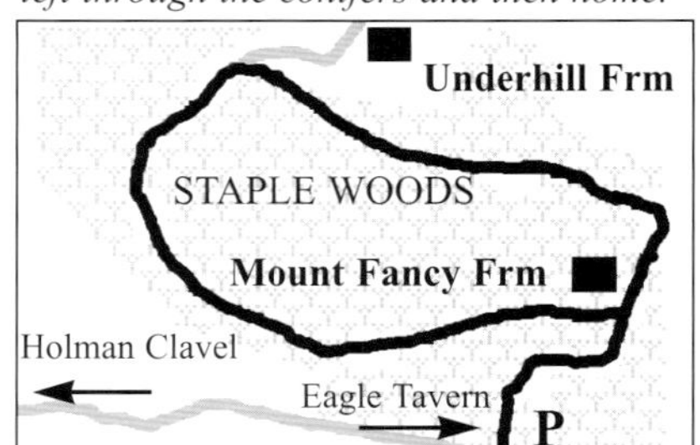

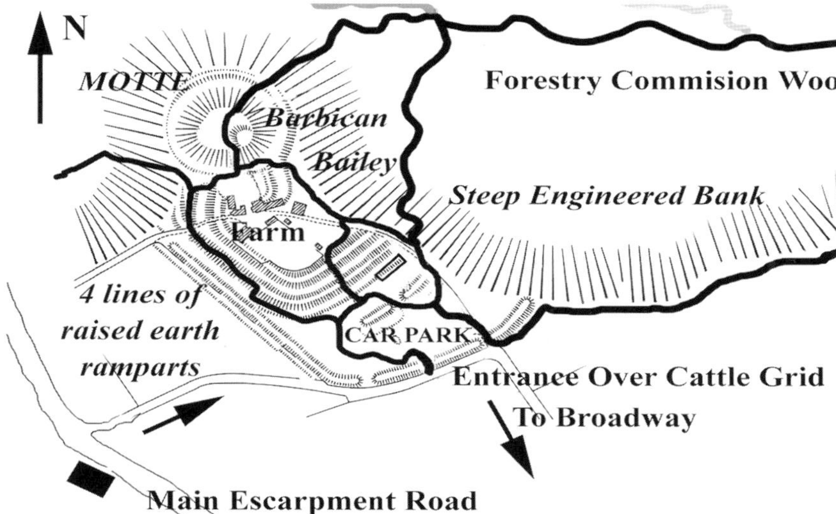

Castle Neroche A Strategic Outpost

It is almost as if no-one wishes you to find **Castle Neroche**! The only signing to it is a rough board sign set in the road side, pointing you towards a 'Nature Walk' off the high scarp road between the Holman Clavel and Eagle Tavern Pubs. What a travesty, when contained within the walls are two or more thousand years of human military history on the Blackdowns. To find Neroche we have to be very careful not to miss the turning. We travel 2 miles past Staple Woods, counting three lanes to pass on our right and the road into Staple Fitzpaine on our left. Directly after this, slow down and start looking out for a narrow lane leading up a hill on your left. There is a pretty cottage opposite on our right with the sign for Neroche almost hidden in the hedge left. Take this left lane and after a quarter of a mile you will find a cattle grid and a gateway to your left.

Any army who controlled the high ground at Neroche, whatever the period were able to police passage to or from the Westcountry very efficiently, with the North Somerset, South Devonshire and Dorset coasts no more than a single days ride away for a complement of horse. A forced route march for soldiers to Minehead or Lyme Regis would take less than two days by foot, even when weighed down with sword, spear and shield. Strangely Neroche is not recorded in the Doomsday book and therefore there is little evidence to classify it as a Bronze, Iron Age or Roman fortification, despite Paleolithic implements, a Bronze age axe and a Roman tile being found within the encampment.

The scale of the fortification is immense and it covers a good half mile from East to West, with fortified tracks continuing even further. There are four high inner banks towering 20ft. above you from the ditch that they form. In the centre of the **Bailey** is a working farm constructed of flint and cherts, built on what was once the all essential rabbit warren mound, just below the **100ft high Norman Motte**.

The Residents of Neroche

The most important person in the known history of **Castle Neroche** is **Count Robert de Mortain,** William the Conqueror's half brother who occupied the fort from 1067. Neroche was similar geographically to the area where Mortain had lived in France and he converted the top of the Motte into a Residence, as well as developing it as a strategic base. He even laid siege to Dunster Castle from here. At the time **Queen Gytha**, King Harold's mother still held Exeter with two of his sons. For a short while, she caused considerable upheaval to Norman plans. However, the Mortain families were no angels themselves when it came to a spot of rebellion. The massive estates the family ran from Montacute were confiscated at the end of the 11th. century, including the Manor at Staple as punishment for leading an uprising themselves. Ironically Dunster Castle at Minehead was to become the Mortain family home for several centuries after. Neroche must have had a special strategic position throughout Blackdown history. It is believed that forces for **Monmouth's Rebellion** must have assembled here and beacons would have warned Taunton in troubled times.

Neroche Farm

Motte at Neroche

The Motte is a massive earthwork. One that would have had originally a wooden keep at the top. This may have been replaced with a stone version. However, Neroche does not easily give up its secrets.

The Castle was used as a garrison for militia in the area throughout the ages. Perhaps, up to 500 men and horse could be stationed here under canvas. It is easy to suppose that the Castle became a regular point of reference for meetings, legal and otherwise. That is, when an army or police force were not in residence.

Inaccessibility and a well centralised position also made the mounds and forest an ideal hideout for the lawless and the vagabond.

Many must have been the hearthside stories of treasure, hoards of smuggled goods hidden in the gullies of Neroche and of the revenue men to tire of waiting and disappear. What tales this place could tell of moonrakers, revenge, highwaymen and gypsies, if only we were able to make it give up the secrets.

The trail is easily followed, well worn and sometimes in poor repair. When you are at the foot of the Motte you may choose to take the long walk by crossing the trail and going down the steps.

To take the shorter route, turn right up the hill onto the wider track, which leads you back up and underneath the great Northern bank, back to the car park.

Staple Fitzpaine, Badgers and Home

We leave our detour to Neroche and retrace our steps to turn right at the cattle grid and down the lane back onto the High Scarp Road. Here we turn right to retrace our journey a quarter of a mile to turn off the Blackdowns into the Tone Vale and the village of ***Staple Fitzpaine****.*

Before the Fitzpaine family took over the original Manor House in the reign of Edward 3rd, the village was then known by the Saxon name of **Staple Brieves**. **St. Peters Church** is almost in perfect harmony with its surroundings, set amongst the Manor house, attendant flint stone cottages and the magnificent scenery of the escarpment leading up to Castle Neroche. A history of wealth and poverty has dogged Staple Manor. The original House burnt to the ground! When rebuilt it was given to **Sir Hugh Popham** in 1600 but less than 100 years later it was used as a poor house. In 1944 the Parish was sold to the Crown and most of the area remains as Crown Estate today.

In addition to a fine Church, Manor House and the flint and chert stone Inn, **The Greyhound**, there are several **'Sarcen stones'** in the village. Large Rocks which do not originate in this geological area. The word 'Staple' means stone. Folklore, says the Devil threw them from Neroche in a fit of spite. Inside the rock is red! To scratch them is said to make them bleed! On the alms houses built by the Pophams is the inscription : -

"These poor to have two pence per week, and a black cloth gown once in two years, which they are obliged, if well, to wear at Church every Sunday : - or forfeit six pence to the clerk!".

Shadows claw at a Bleeding Stone

The Greyhound Inn originated as the Hunting Lodge for the Royal Forests of Neroche. The Inn maintains the tradition of being a fine hostelry, with en-suite bed & breakfast accommodation, a traditional bar, a hands on landlord and a high quality restaurant, which serves special recipes not to be found elsewhere. *From the Inn we turn right out of the car park to continue on to the Hamlet of* ***Badger Street****.* The name derived from the many disenfranchised male brocks coming down off the Blackdowns, through the cluster of cottages to search for a mate.

The same may well have been applied to young Blackdown men on simular quests, especially at the local Saturday night hops in the valley village halls throughout the 1960's, where even then the social and cultural differences between the high hill and valley folk gave cause for some very tactful courtships. Some to verge on the secretive at least!

"Don't you have any goin's on with them Black Folk, Maid!" Them's will 'a do 'ee more 'arm than good, I tell 'eee!

It is with this interesting speculation that we leave our second route to discovering the Blackdowns as we turn right at Taunton National Hunt Race Course over the M5 and home.

Although 12 long miles separate **Cullompton** from **Wellington** the travelling distance these days between them is no more than ten minutes. Each town is closely linked by the M5 motorway and the old A38, now demoted to the B3181. However, the similarities do not end there. Both have fine Churches and a diversity of industry, with it's roots lying in cloth, wool and agriculture, resulting in a long developed partnership with the people of the Blackdowns. Therefore, it is appropriate to give you choices of how to discover the Northwest Route of the Blackdowns from both of these towns. **From Wellington** directions start from the centre of town to head South from the original by pass of the A38/ B3181, under the M5 and up the Wellington Monument Road to join route **No. 3** by crossing the High Scarpe Road towards Hemyock. **From Cullompton,** the route is slightly more arduous. We must travel along the old A38/ new B3181 into the village of Willand, where just West of The Halfway House Pub we turn right towards Uffculme, with our first stop at one of the main attractions on the Blackdowns, the Historic **Coldharbour Woollen Mill at Uffculme.**

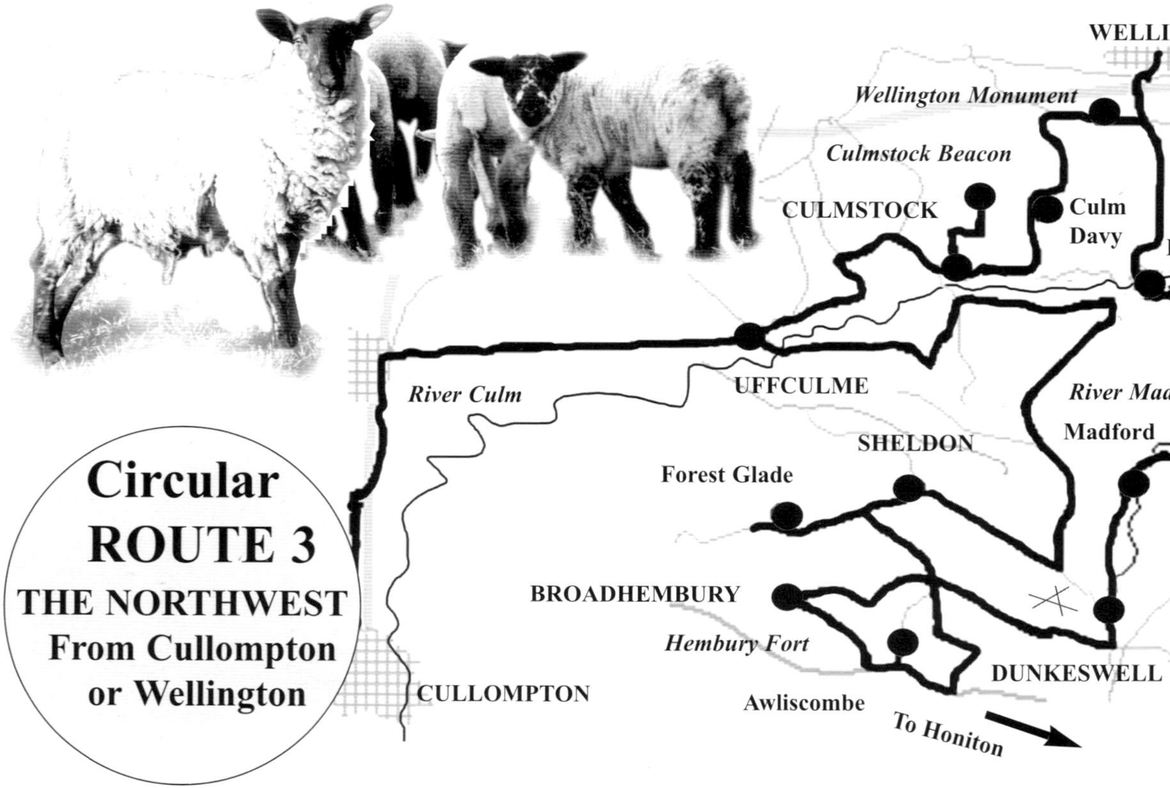

Uffculme Wool Town

The route from the B3181 at Willand to the Mill Town of **Uffculme** is as straight as a dye for one mile. The town's modern name has not changed much in form, from the day it was first recorded in the Doomsday Book. The Church of **St. Mary the Virgin** has the largest rood screen in Devonshire. The Northern arcade and arch to the modern tower may be dated to the mid 13 th. century. Inside is perhaps the most colourful tomb in the area. That of Sir William Walrond who is painted both red and blue, whilst his son and wife are visually preserved in green.

The most outstanding cultural feature of Uffculme is the wooden roofed shelter with benches below, at the centre of the village square. The elaborate wooden artifact is called **the Shambles**. Here has been the focal point of this village life for some centuries! Conveniently placed on an elevated position near two public houses, T**he George** and the **The Ostler**, it was ideal for holding auctions and public meetings throughout the ages. One must wonder how many first tentative romantic meetings or proposals of marriage evolved at this siting of ancient woodwork.

Wool was the most stable of trading currencies throughout the middle ages and this prosperity continued well into the Victorian era, where fleeces were a major commodity for trade with European and world markets. **Coldharbour Mill Museum** is the local, public expression for the long association between this small town, the Blackdown Hills and the sheep which roamed here.

Water power converted to steam with the coming of the industrial revolution and with it the wool industry at Coldharbour reached its peak in the mid 17 hundreds. Over 170 people were employed on the looms within the red local brick Walls.

Coldharbour Mill is now an important Heritage Site, where exhibitions and demonstrations reveal the links between farmer and the wealth of the Wool and Weaving industries. Cold Harbour Mill is also a cracking good day out, with guided tours, a beam steam engine, a restaurant and excellent walks along the Culm River to reveal Uffculme as a Victorian Mill Town in miniature.

CULMSTOCK

The next village on our route is ***Culmstock.*** *The Saxons Called it* ***Columbstocke*** *(A stockade by the Columb river). There are two routes to finding it from Uffculme. To avoid duplicity we travel the Northern lane by taking the left uphill road from the triangle which forms the village square of Uffculme. This leads us past Five Fords Farm and Spicelands, where less than 300 yds on we turn right at the crossroads to travel through* **Prescott***. Just below Woodbine Farm is a hall dated 1670 , that was a Meeting House for the Society of Friends. The lane parallels the Culm River to join the B3391 from Maiden Down. A right turn takes us over the fine arched stone bridge into* ***Culmstock.***

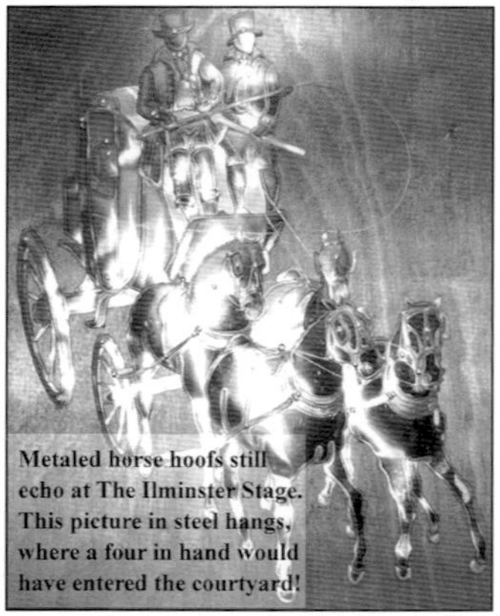

Metaled horse hoofs still echo at The Ilminster Stage. This picture in steel hangs, where a four in hand would have entered the courtyard!

Again, it was wool at the heart of prosperity here. In 1396 a Culmstock wool merchant was reputed to be doing more business than any other of his kind in the whole of England. Just as the village has two public Houses, **'The Ilminster Stage'** and **'The Culm Valley Inn'**, it also has two famous sons. The foremost of which, was **Frederick Temple**, who became **Archbishop of Canterbury**. He was educated with **Richard Doddridge Blackmore**, the Culmstock boy who became the famous author of **'Lorna Doone'**.

It is not without some wonder that Mr. Blackmore may have based some of the characters in 'Lorna Doone', on those keen edged Blackdown people from this locality, he knew so well as a child. He certainly used his local knowledge in his lesser known book **'Perlycross'**, with his story set in the area - '*where the yew tree grew in the tower of the flint built Church of All Saints, at Perliton'*- (Culmstock) -*'with its head overtopping the battlements and scraping the scroll of the South East vane'.*

That yew tree still stands high against the winter gales today. In the Church there is a 15th cent. velvet cope in gold woven by women of the parish. Literally 100's of **'Comstocks'** from America visit the village annually to trace their roots back from an 18th century immigrant who came from the village. His name 'Culmstock' was accidentally misspelt to become Comstock by an immigration official in The New World. Seemingly there are over 30,000 Comstocks now living in the USA today. Good strong genes in these Blackdown Men! *There is a 3 mile circular walk from the* ***Culm Valley Inn.*** *You will find the footpath at the bridge. The path takes you along the river for one mile to Five Fords. Bear left over the footbridge. You can carry on right to Uffculme if you wish to return to Culmstock, then climb left up Ratsash Lane towards the main road. Keeping left past Ivy Cottages and onto the main road. Go left past Home Farm through Craddock to turn back to the River Culm, down the footpath at Lowmoor Farm, through Southey Barton then left to Woodhayne Barton and home.*

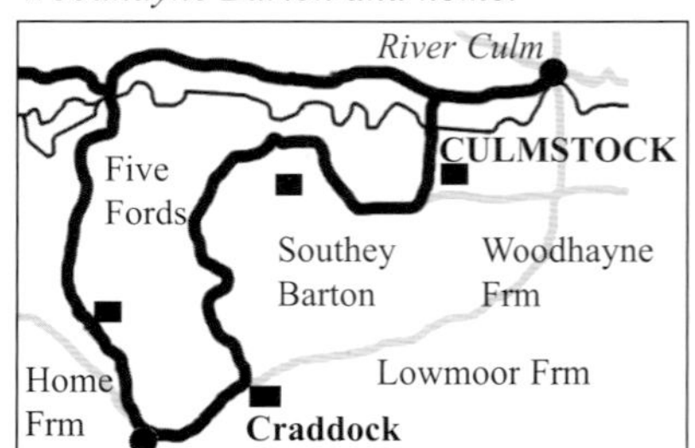

CULMSTOCK and to The Beacon

As we leave Culmstock it is interesting to note that both pub names follow the tradition of transport. **The Culm Valley Inn**, recently the Railway Inn and **The Ilminster Stage Inn**. **'The Stage'** was the Posting Stop for the Mail Coach, where a four in hand would test the best of drivers to negotiate the narrow entrance into the stabling courtyard opposite the Church. This is now blocked off to form part of the friendly locals bar and up and coming restaurant.

The Culm Valley Inn grew prosperous with the arrival of the steam train in what was then a very commercial town. The line even survived Mr. Beecham and remained one of the last regular passenger and freight services to run under British Rail in the Westcountry, powered by the 0-6-0 DM, 'Tivvy Bumper'. Oh! that delicious whiff of coal furnessed steam coming out the stack on a frosty Culm Vale morning. The pub holds to the tradition well and it is an authentic step back in time with good food and ale on hand. *We get ourselves to the Beacon by returning the way we came to the fork near the school, where we branch off right, up the hill for a quarter mile to a 'T" junction.*

We turn right and travel for another quarter of a mile until we come to the track that leads left to the telephone relay aerial, below Blackdown Common. It is, perhaps best to leave your transport neatly parked, as turning is difficult at the top. The climb up to the Common is steep and the exposed flints will be hard on falling knees. The escarpment is a flint knappers paradise. The beacon still stands from the days it was lit in warning of the Spanish Armada. Shaped like a Pizza oven, what we are really seeing is a shelter for men and a dry store for wood, with fire baskets going up through the hole in the roof supported by a pole and a ladder to reach them.

Tivvy Bumper at Culmstock Level Crossing

BLACK DOWN COMMON

You will find a doorway into the inside of the beacon. There is a large hole in the roof with two windows set in alignment with Holcombe Rogus and Smeatharpe. The volunteer firesmen would have had shelter and plentiful dry wood to feed the two fire baskets set on the pole above them at first sight of a signal on the horizon. Beacons were lit here

again in 1998 on the Blackdowns to bring attention to the plight of the farmers. Once again there are threats to this land from Europe.

On reaching the top of **Black Down Common**, there are so many tracks it is quite easy to become lost, unless you make good your bearings. The radio mast set in Whitehall Plantation to the West of Wellington Monument, is the most visible fix. *There is a fine circular 3 mile walk, giving fabulous views from the top and along the base of the escarpment.* Some surrounding farmers are attempting to improve the land here for more grazing. Perhaps any further enclosures of this land should cease. Here is the last look at what the majority of the high Blackdowns were really like until a century and a half ago. There is a very special ecology here. Wildlife and rare plants are threatened with each burning, as well as also causing considerable inconvenience to the fire services.

Behind the Beacon near the marker a track leads you gently down. Follow this for a quarter of a mile and it will join the public footpath. This leads you right across the top of the common up to a plantation. Take the track leading left to take you into the bottoms at the top of Green Lane. Bear left again and follow the track for a long mile to Purchas Farm. You will find a bridle way on your left, to bring you home just below the Beacon.

Storytelling wooden sculpture overlooks the Culm Vale

Black Down Common is the most isolated part of The Blackdowns. The two square miles of heathland are untouched by metalled roads. Because of this we must return to Culmstock to find our way to Hemyock. *On returning to the outskirts stop at the four cross way with the school on your right. Take the left hand road to parallel the River Culm past the old mill. This pleasant lane will take you for two and a half miles into* ***Hemyock.*** *For those who wish to include the Wellington Monument (Page 42) on their route, turn off left through* ***Culm Davy*** *for 2 miles to climb up to the scarp road and turn right. To return to Hemyock turn right off the scarp road through Simonsburrow and Rosemary Lane.*

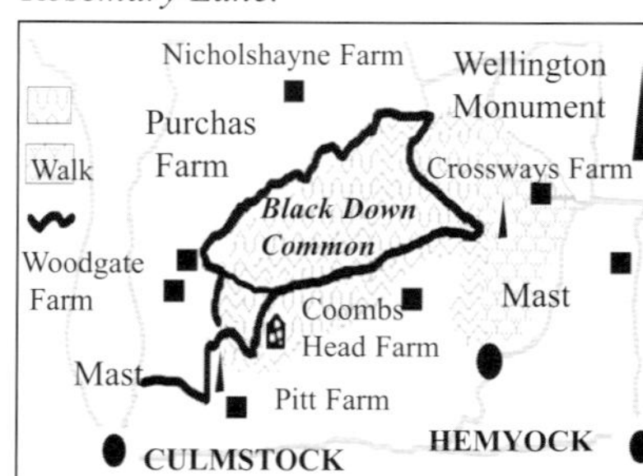

HEMYOCK

The first thing to come to our notice are the buildings of the St.Ival Milk Processing Plant at Withy Lane. We turn right through the complex which once employed 140 people but is now closed. Short term gains for a few, long term social and environmental disharmony for many! Oh! the wisdom of profiteering for shareholders? The raised wooden walkway on the near side is a solution to elevating pedestrians beyond oversized vehicles and the flood waters of the Culm River.

This town had the pre-Doomsday title of **'Hamock'**. The Normans improved the Manor house with turrets, which with additions of battlements in 1380 formed a formidable stronghold. During Cromwell's brief administration, the Castle was used to imprison Royalist sympathisers under the direction of **Sir John Popham**. Inmates included the vicar of Upottery, **James Burnard**, who refused to use the Presbyterian Directory. This use of the castle stuck hard with the Royalists and when they were restored to power in 1660, King Charles 2nd endorsed the castle's destruction by **Lord Poulett**. Little remains of the original fortifications today, although the property is opened to the public on bank holidays and by appointment.

Hemyock lost The Culm Valley branch line only a decade ago. It was opened in 1876, when Hemyock was another industrial hub for the Blackdowns. New housing estates rest uneasily amongst the relics of a bustling historical past, to whisper that nothing, including plentiful petrol, lasts for ever. However, Hemyock still at the centre of the social calendar for the Hills, with an annual carnival, a pantomime and it was in this valley that the idea of Young Farmers Clubs was born.

The Catherine Wheel Inn, is at this town's centre and supports an excellent restaurant and a welcoming watering hole. The Catherine Wheel was the emblem for an order of medieval knights, to which a 14 th. century chapel was dedicated in the **Church of St. Mary's** opposite. The church was rebuilt in the late 19 th. century with the tower built purposely low at the demands of the owners of the castle, (The Pophams). Powerful people to demand that their private home should not be overshadowed by the house of God. The town sports several general purpose shops, a hairdressers, a Post Office and is the home base of the Blackdown Medical Practice. **The Victorian Memorial** is priceless, in that it boxes in the town pump. Not only does it celebrate the Coronation of Queen Victoria and Edward seventh but also an end to the Boer War in 1902.

MADFORD & DUNKESWELL ABBEY

The journey from Hemyock to Dunkeswell Abbey is fraught with the danger of getting lost. In order to succeed in finding the Abbey we leave Hemyock at the Memorial to Queen Victoria, with the main street to our rear and travel up the narrowing lane to Moorhayes Cross, a mile away. At Moorhayes we turn left down into the pretty Madford River Valley. Just before the river there is a road leading off sharply to our right. We take this and after 200 yards or so, we find the hamlet of thatched cottages attendant to the Abbey.

The beauty is such here that there is little wonder why **William Brewer** in the early twelve hundreds, wished for this pretty spot to be his final resting place. Brewer, The High Sheriff of Devon and Cornwall was one of the Barons who signed the **Magna Carta** and helped to arrange the release of **Richard Coeur de Lion** from imprisonment. Stone coffins thought to be of both he and his wife remain in the modern **Church of the Holy Trinity** in the Abbey grounds. This was built by the **Simcoe's** of Wolford Lodge on returning from Canada in 1842 from stones retrieved from the Abbey.

Brewer gave permission to the **Cistercian Monks of Forde Abbey** to build this most historically important site on the Blackdowns. The self contained Cistercian Monks were semi vegetarians, only eating fish meat from the numerous ponds they maintained. Wool was their wealth coinage! A fulling mill for the washing and beating of cloth, the earliest in the country is recorded nearby. There are still some traces of the Abbey walls remaining. There are also some 13th. century tiles with the earliest known English representations of elephants in their design in the Church. Many a stone from the Abbey might be found in the walls of neighbouring farm buildings, where good use was made of them after the Dissolution.

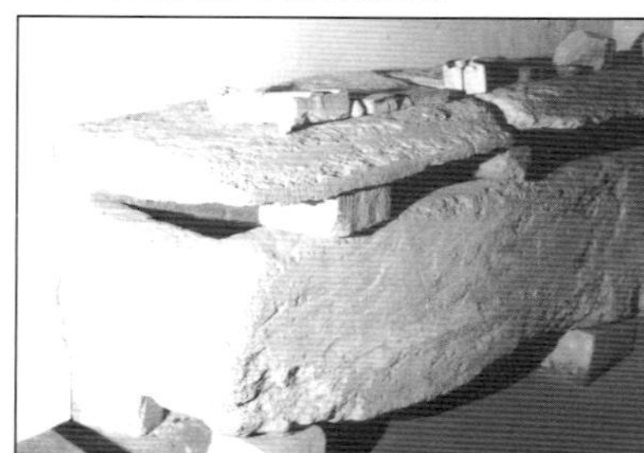

DUNKESWELL

On entering Dunkeswell from the Abbey Road there appears to be a typical Devonshire Village, with working farms at it's centre, a red telephone box, the modern **Church of St Nicholas**, thatched cottages and a traditional pub, **'The Royal Oak'.** Cows can be met coming up from the milking parlour at Church Farm and Christmas trees can be bought straight from the farmer at Yuletide. Yet it is **Dunkeswell** which has become the most progressive village of the Blackdowns. Over 500 modern homes have been built where a wartime camp and hospital once stood and there is a growing complex of modern industrial buildings just above the village. The blame at, or gratitude for, can be directed towards the Ministry of Defence who designated the flat plain at Dunkeswell to become the **U. S. Navy Air Facility FAW7** from 1943 to 1945. The population of less than 200 swelled to over 5000 with three squadrons of Liberator PB4Y-1 submarine search and destroy bombers, their aircrew and attendant ground staff to support them. **FAW7** operations were paramount to defeating the U-Boat menace in the Western Approaches. The 183 officers and men who died in action from here are remembered at the **Church of St. Nicholas** on a plaque above the organ given to the parish by the American Veterans.

Control Tower 1944

The Airmans Memorial

The runways have since become a centre of excellence for flying. There is the very successful **Devon School of Flying** where both lessons and flights can be arranged**.** With the infamous **Dawn Patrol** you can experience the nostalgia of a fully aerobatic biplane and there is a **Parachute School** based at the airfield, which holds the Royal Marine record for the highest stack. In addition there is a **Microlight Club**, a Rally School and regular **Go-Kart** Meetings at the weekends. The **Memorial Museum** is dedicated to The **US Navy FAW 7** and it holds fascinating insights into the airfield's past history. At the entrance is the **Air Centre Restaurant & Playpark** with the **Bunker Cafe** in a Nissen hut along Marcus Road.

Dunkeswell a Centre of Changes

One cannot disguise the enormous impact the second World War has had at Dunkeswell with three great runways and buildings sprawling over several hundred acres of the 900 ft. high plateaux. There were however, two former occasions when Dunkeswell was at the centre of massive changes on the Blackdowns.

The 1st. was in the 13th. century when the Cistercian Monks became established with several manors in the area, encouraging the valley land to be further enclosed and an infrastructure of drovers lanes developed between the estates and routes of pilgrimage.

A great example of this gentle shaping of the landscape is the lovely waterside landscape at **Fishponds House**. Here you can stay or camp in the Summer months around a complex that sports a fine restaurant, a bar and several carefully stocked ponds, where you can fish. To find **Fishponds** from the old village bare left at the 'T' junction at Highfields and travel East down an ever winding lane, for a mile.

The 2nd. occasion of change at Dunkeswell was during the late 18th. century when Upper Canada's retiring First Lieutenant Governor, General, John Graves Simcoe returned to Wolford Lodge. Distantly related to William Brewer his experience of taming wide open spaces encouraged him to enclose 12,000 acres of the high 'Common Land' into manageable farms, with large modern fields displacing many independent commoners to leave the area or become workers.

In 1943 it was the Air Ministry Director of Works who requisitioned several of these farms under the Emergency Powers (Defence) Act and a Highway Closing order was served on several of the country roads. These were considerably widened and improved by the Americans. It took the land owners until 1945 to settle the compensation for their land and buildings and then only at 1939 prices! However, the modern day changes at Dunkeswell are fast becoming cause for environmental concern, in that whilst making an all important centre for local work and housing, the planners have not provided an adequate road infrastructure to service the traffic visiting the industrial sites and roads are degrading under the heavy traffic and articulated lorries.

To find Walford Chapel we bare right at the 'T' junction past the **Highfield Shopping** complex with its **Garage, Post Office, Doctors Surgery, Hairdressers, Supermarket** and **Fish and Chip Shop**.

To visit **Wolford Chapel** is to almost visit **Canada** itself, as the deeds to the chapel and the land it stands were given to the people of Ontario in 1966 by Sir Geoffrey Harmsworth. **General Simcoe**, his wife, and several of his eleven children are buried in the graveyard. In the nave of the **Church of St Nicholas**, Dunkeswell, there are also six corbels of angels carved by Henry Ezard, each in portrait a representation of the General's six daughters.

Awliscombe and Hembury Fort

To continue our route from Walford Chapel we turn right off the chapel lane onto the Dunkeswell to Honiton road. After 300 meters we come to Limers Cross. We have the choice to go into Honiton and go to Awliscombe via the A373, or take the narrow, pretty lane off to our Right. This takes us over the steep western escarpment through the ancient woodland of St.Cyres Hill and leads us directly into the main road village of Awliscombe.

This little village has a pub, **the Awliscombe Arms,** nestling just below the 15th. century Church of St Michael and all Angels. A Church reputed to be built on the site of a pagan temple. The font dates from around 1450 and the chapel has parts dating back to the 1200's. The Tudor stained glass windows are exemplary. From here the most Westerly Iron Age fortification of Hembury lies a mere two miles away. From Awliscombe we travel for just over a mile along the A373, to look out for the first turning right after the steep climb past Hembury Fort House. 300 yards up the steep lane will bring you to a wide verge where you can park your vehicle. Pathways to the fort lead out on your right to leave you to ramble at will.

A Friend of Awliscombe Church

Hembury Fort

Hembury is some 900 feet above sea level and was once a Neolithic Village dating at around 3,000 BC. These early people had learnt to domesticate animals and grew crab apples, wheat and barley in small fields below the steep slopes of the fort. They were succeeded by the Beaker folk from Western Europe, so called because of the shape of their pottery. Another group of people, the Urn Folk superseded them to trade as far away as Ireland. Excavations by the University of Exeter show that the massive hill fort was also probably occupied by the Romans some 600 year later. The Fort is protected by two deep ditches on the Northern side, with steeply descending natural inclines into the Southern and Western flanks.

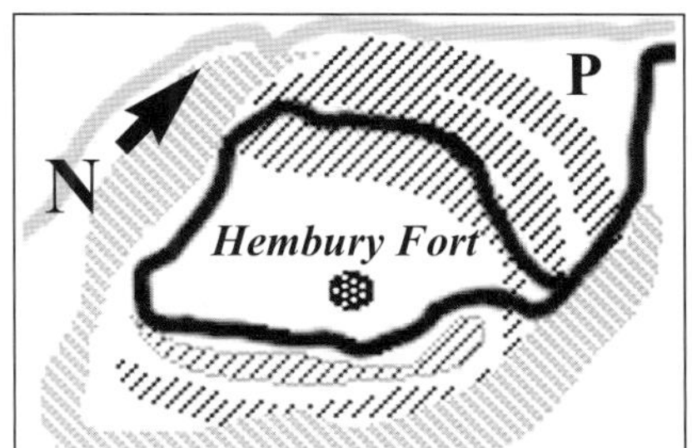

BROADHEMBURY

The Drewe Arms

*From **Hembury Fort** we retrace our steps to the A373, turn right and then after 100 yards, right again onto the lane that will take us to the best kept secret on the Blackdowns.* '**Broadhembury**'. This delightful village is a classic example of a mediaeval nucleated settlement with Saxon roots. A major reason for the survival of so much cob and thatch is that the properties have remained in the ownership of two families named **Drewe,** for many centuries. The first was that of Edward Drewe who bought the Manor from the Dunkeswell Abbey estate in 1603. The second was the Drewe family of Castle Drogo in the Teign Valley, who purchased the estate earlier this century. We must congratulate the integrity of these families for the preservation of the unique whole. At the centre of the Village is the **Drewe Arms.** A caringly maintained expression of a traditional Inn eased gently into the demands of the late 20th. century. An evening meal, lunch, or a snack here is not only a delight but also an encounter with culinary excellence. The magnificent tower of the **Church of St. Andrews**, maintains a serene dignity over the unspoilt cluster of 14th. century thatched cottages.

Broadhembury was quite the centre for this part of the Blackdowns at one time, having a three day fair to celebrate the Assumption of St Mary. Also, the Composer of the hymn **'Rock of Ages'**, the **Rev. Augustus Toplady** was the Vicar of St. Andrews from 1768 to 1788. *To walk the area go over the stone stream bridge to follow the lane for a mile. This ends up as a track. At the 'T' take a left up the hill. This will take you through the woods from where **The Devon & Somerset Gliding Club** operates. Keep right at the track and onto the tarmac lane. Opposite a farm track, look for a footpath across the fields on your right to join the steep lane down into Broadhembury, (4 miles). A right at the 'T' will bring you along the lanes to Stafford Barton and down the hill into Broadhembury, (2 miles).*

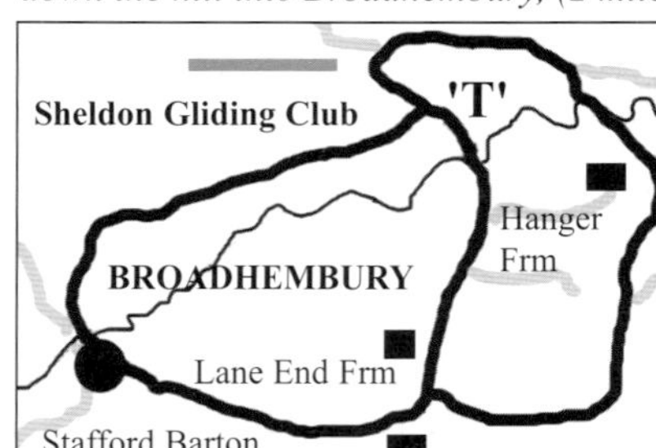

North Hill & Sheldon, a very Secret Village

We leave Broadhembury with the Church on our right and tackle the steep hill towards Dunkeswell for one and a half miles, to turn left at the first cross roads. It is difficult to find a place to stop here but on your right, hidden deep under bracken and furze, there is a tumulus waiting to be discovered at Dunkeswell Turbury.

Our route continues across the Western side of the Dunkeswell Plateaux and over Ponchy Down. After a mile a private track leads left off to the ***Devon & Somerset Glider Club*** *at North Hill.* There is a woodland walk alongside the take off and landing strip and it makes for a fascinating afternoon watching the aircraft being towed into the sky or sometimes thrown into it by a massive cable winch. On good days, when the thermals are right pilots seem to hang in the air for hours.

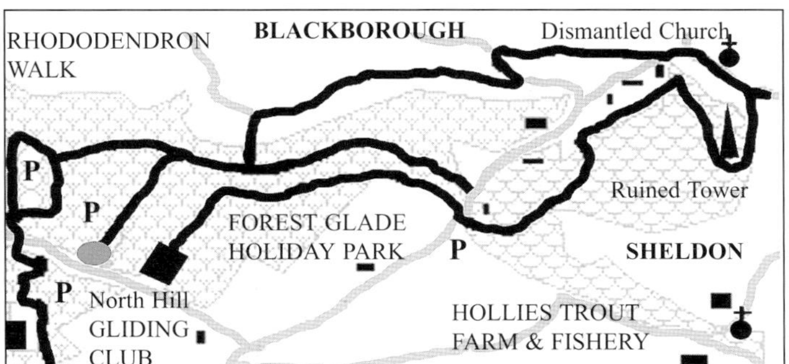

Just beyond the gliding, we find the **Forest Glade International Caravan & Camping Park** at Forest Glade House. Set in woodland, holiday makers have a marvellous base from which to explore the many tracks and walks, through Knowles Woods and Black Down. The most excellent of which follows the old Bridle Way to **Blackborough**.

The area was known as 'the Sythstone Hills', where Cornishmen came to mine the whetstone for several centuries until the trade died through cheaper Spanish imports. The road to the tiny village of **Sheldon** is off to our right and leads down to the delightful wayside Church of **St. James the Greater.** A footpath leads through the Church yard to the fields. The tower of the Church is original and the font is Norman. Nearby, **Hollies Trout Farm & Fishery** will rent you a rod for fly fishing trout in carefully stocked ponds. Coarse fishing is also available.

Return to the Road through to Blackborough to lead you off the escarpment and onto Uffculme and home to Cullompton, to end route No3.

HONITON is our fourth town serving the Blackdowns. On a Saturday morning it still retains the flavour of a mediaeval market town with traders lining the streets with covered stalls. The right to hold a market dates to the 13th century and if it hadn't been for a succession of dreadful fires, Honiton would have remained a superb example of a Westcountry town, preserved throughout the ages. Even so, you can spot the small extensions into the roofs which were accommodations for the apprentice weavers and lace makers, to gives us an idea of how the town grew up around the cloth industry. Many of the skills of serge and lace making was brought to the town by the **Lollards** (A pious group of non-conformists), escaping the religious persecutions of Flanders.

Today, Honiton or 'Honey Town' is a hive of antiques businesses, with the High Street really putting itself out to cater for the visitor and local alike. It sports a selection of tea rooms, restaurants, pubs, gift and traditional shops, with a Museum and an Information Centre in the Library.

The museum is housed in the old chapel of All Hallows, the oldest building to have survived the fires. Inside are some real indicators to the geology of the area and besides examples of the wonderful Honiton Lace and the poverty of those who made it, there are the bones of an elephant, a reindeer and an hippopotamus uncovered by the excavations for the Honiton by-pass in 1965.

- And what a blessing to the town - that was !

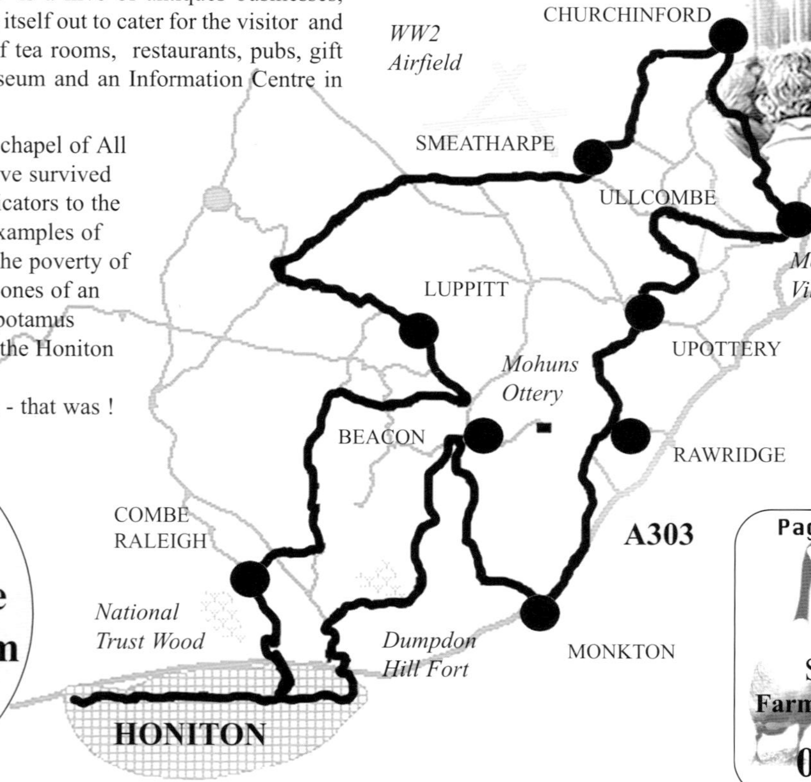

Circular ROUTE 4 The Heart of the Blackdowns from HONITON

COMBE RALEIGH

Honiton is a town that must be walked to be properly appreciated. It does so much draw the stomach of a person. The smell of fresh bread, the lure of a wet fish shop, a homemade Ice Cream Parlour and a butcher who still cuts your joint to choice. Such is the character of a town with one foot deeply in a tangible past, yet also supports the choice of two Supermarkets. The people have an insatiable taste for the best of local country produce, served up by a host of individual businesses. By so doing they protect their culture and the local jobs that go with it.

Our journey starts by pointing ourselves to the east along the High Street, where we look out on the left hand side just after The Red Cow Inn, for ***Fielding Lane****. We turn left down this narrow road that looks if it might lead us absolutely nowhere. Not to worry, for after a few hundred yards we tunnel beneath the by-pass of the A303, to immediately transcend into the green and lush countryside and over the serpentine* ***River Otter****. After a half mile the road rises into* ***Tracy wood****. This makes for a delightful sanctuary and is carefully preserved for us by the National Trust. The side of the road provides a few places to park, if you squeeze in tight to the hedge.*

Field Art

There is a pathway leading into the wood and a bench from which to enjoy the privilege, beauty and peace encapsulated here. A little further down the lane we come to a farm which is the first outpost of the Village of **Combe Raleigh**.

The village was known as Combawton in the time of Henry the 3rd and later on Combe Cofyn, Combe Matthew and finally Combe Rawleigh. The name changes, apparently susceptible to whatever notable families lived there at the time. Several prehistoric Burial Mounds were found just North of the Village in 1960's, but they are not shown on most O/S maps.

The Church of **St. Nicholas de Bari**, has a 14th. century tower with an unusual outer staircase, with walls of Blackdown flint with the pillars and arcade of Beer Stone. The Abbot's House was built in 1790 and was used as a prison camp in WW1. At the centre of the village is a Chantry House dated 1498 with an open roof and carved oak screens.

LUPPITT

Before we leave Combe Raleigh, a word of warning about becoming 'Pixie Led'. This will probably happen to you no matter how good you may be at reading maps or these directions. If you get lost then turn a pocket inside out, or if that is inconvenient a coat or shirt will do. You will find a way home soon. If you are out walking and lost just call out loudly, "Persons a'lost", and someone will find you, some day. The thing to be very careful of is not to step in the Pixie rings, known locally as 'gallitraps'. To stand where the Pixies dance will probably lead you to die by hanging! They say Pixies are more mischievous than their delicate counterparts, the fairies, although personally I can never tell the difference. However, one method of damage limitation is not to pick the greater stichwort plant, another is not to drink to much, or at best, non at all before travelling the twisting and turning lanes of the Blackdown Hills with wheeled transport.

Our Journey will take us over the crossroads with the Dunkeswell/ Honiton Road and deep into the valley beneath the mysterious knowle of trees and steep earthern battlements of Dumpton Hill.

We come to the Hamlet of Stonehayes to go over the cross way to ***Greenway Farm,*** *which along with neighbouring* ***Shapscombe,*** *was mentioned at Doomsday. Here we bear right into the bottoms, to turn left up into the steeply inclined village of* ***Luppitt.***

Luppitt's most famous character is Mary the Landlady of the **Luppitt Inn** for many years. This pub is a real Blackdown pub. Nothing fancy, no fake woodwork, no flashy beer dispensers. In fact its just like walking into someone's home a century past. The last of the many Blackdown houses which would have sold ale and cider. Opposite is the idyllic home, which houses the Post Office.

The collection of cottages, many dating back to the 14th. century, are enhanced by the 13th. century tower of **St. Marys Church**, standing high on the steep hillside. You can find parking at the village hall or just above the Church in a car park marked by a standing stone set deep into the wall. The views of the steep sided valley are truly magnificent. The setting, idyllic!

The Church has a fine Devon wagon roof an extraordinary font with unusual carvings, and contains a strange glass object, thought to be a sound amplifier. However, the countryside surrounding Luppitt is the greatest attraction. The clear peaty springs at the head of the little valley provide the water to make the famous **Otter Ale**. It is from Luppitt that we can take a superb walk over **Hartridge** past **Mohens Ottery.**

Hartridge and Hense Moor

Walk No (1). The route to ***Hense Moor*** *starts from the bottom of Luppitt just below the village hall at a signed footpath. We go left over the field to a footbridge and again left along a track to Brook Cottage. Turn right with the sign onto a sometimes very wet path that goes up through brackens and woods for a mile. The path leads down into the bottoms and over the Otter's ford and up some really rough territory to Mathays Farm, now a home to the famous* ***Otter Brewery****. (The footpath here is due for re routeing: Please have respect when going this way, it is a working area). After skirting the Brewery go through the fields to Hillend Farm. Go through the farmyard and onto the tarmac road, leading west below Hartridge, to turn right and back into Luppitt.*

Walk No (2).The route to **Hartridge** is to leave Luppitt up the steep tarmacadium road towards **Beacon**. This brings you up the steep incline to bare right along the ridge road into the Hamlet. Just before the first cottage on your left is a track up onto the top of the Hartridge where there is a tumuli with great views over to Luppitt. Take this if you feel like a detour but return to the three cross way and take the first left at the flower filled cottage gardens at **Beacon**. This lane dips into the Otter valley for a quarter of a mile. Take a left turn at the "T" Junction past **Pound Farm** towards **Mohuns Ottery**.

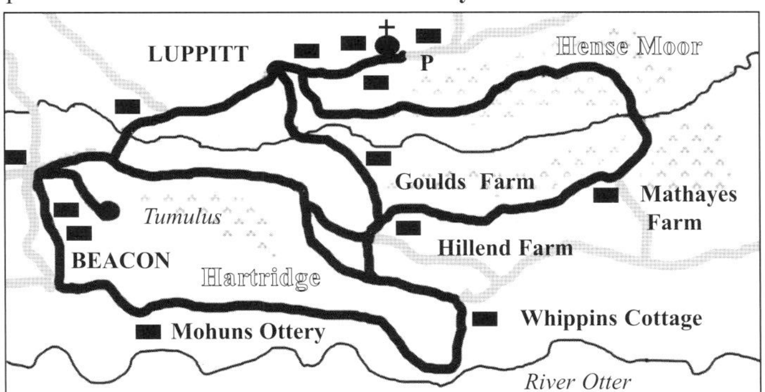

Just before **Mohuns** take the foot path on your left, down a half mile of track to take a left up the hill past Whippins Cottage to exit onto **Luppitt Common**. Follow the tarmac road under Hartridge and then double back right on the road to Hillend Farm. At Goulds Farm there is a footpath into Luppitt.

To continue Route (4), we travel with Luppitt Church on our left to the Dunkeswell/Culmhead road. We bare right for two miles past the B&B at ***'Jacks House'****, to the wide open spaces of* ***Upottery Airfield*** *from which 81 Assault Gliders and their parent Dakotas took off with men of the 506th P.I.R. on the evening of 5th. June 1944 (D-Day) to the historic and fateful drop near St. Mere-Eglise.*

Smeatharpe and the Airfield

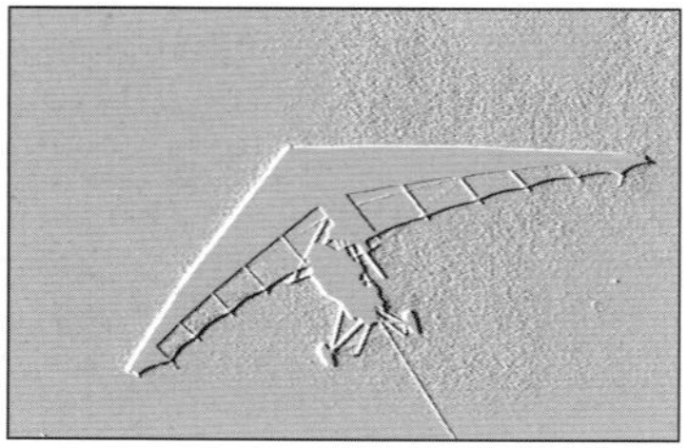

As we pass by the perimeters of the old Airfield at our left there is the stadium where 1970's World Champion Banger Racing Champion Kevin Stack cut his teeth and once a fortnight, on Sundays from Spring to Autumn, the Oval track becomes host to both **Hot Rod and Banger Racing** for Devon and Somerset.

Some locals wave their hands in anguish that such an activity should take place on the Blackdowns but the stadium has been in existence since the 1960's and it is indeed an essential part of the diverse choices of activities, which take place here today.

The East/West runway is also home to a group of model aircraft makers; an ideal training ground for HGV lorry drivers and the NW/ SE runway also plays host to hangliding enthusiasts. They might take you up, for a donation to the Air Ambulance! All activities which take place here are by the kind permission of the land owners.

Smeatharpe 1998

Smeatharpe 1944 With Pub Sign removed

The third runway is in part the public road to **Bolham Water**.

The airfield was a staging post for allied American troops and was used as a ferrying depot for supplies and wounded soldiers during 1944/45. The arrival of Black American soldiers near D-Day is well etched into the memories of local people. In addition, U.S.Navy FAW7 operations flew out from here when runways there deteriorated. The derelict Control Tower, Operations Block and some of the auxiliary buildings are still part of the visible landscape today. At the Eastern end of the complex lies the hamlet of Smeatharpe. A sleepy settlement left with the memories of once having two pubs, a turnpike gate and a village school, which doubled as Church on Sundays. It still has a shop on the main road, where fruit, plants and vegetables don't suffer the cost of middle men and are guaranteed fresh and mostly local. You might also meet a shire horse, and a very happy dog!

CHURCHINFORD A SECOND VISIT

The Blackdowns have often been a place where people might come to escape persecution. The very active **Newhouse Baptist Church** nearby at Smeatharpe is good evidence of this. In the latter 17th. century, during the religious persecutions of the '5 mile Act', with Smeatharpe being removed by 7 miles from any corporate town, many Brethren willingly travelled the 21 miles from Tiverton and beyond to worship here on Sundays.

Newhouse Baptist Church Sunday 10.55 am.

We travel on for one mile after the ***Smeatharpe Farm Shop,*** *to turn right down Red Lane. This brings us to the six crossway at Churchinford's centre. We have been here before. (P 48).* The Baptist chapel adjoining **Myrtle Cottage** in Churchinford, has the distinction of being only the second of it's like to have a bell. A certain Captain White of Royston House fell out with the Church of England Vicar, who was found hunting on his land outside of his company. In revenge the captain allowed the Brethren to build a chapel to serve the needs of a then, very large village, providing the brethren rang the bell regularly to remind the vicar he had lost some of his flock.

"Chuchinford was a market town when Exeter was a fuzzy down".

Churchinford is special today in that it still has a diverse and balanced population of youth, families and elderly. Future economic and environmental planning decisions will determine whether this can continue. Does the village expand without encouraging industries to support a working community, with the risk that commuting to work might not be a tenable option in the next 30 years? Or do we cease building new homes here altogether, where without growth, the shops, the pub, the Church and eventually the spirit of the village might die?

There are two routes to walk off a lunch at the **York Inn**. *No1. (3 miles) to Otterhead Lakes. Walk along the Taunton Road past the Village Hall for half a mile. A public footpath leads through a gateway on your right. (Pathfind 1 on P 29).* Walk No2. To Mediaeval Ruins. (5 miles). Leave the York Inn and go down Moor Lane into the Otter Bottoms. Bare right after the little bridge to a concrete flood ford. Take a left over the cattle grid to Watchford Farm, to bare right and then left past Stout Farm to Higher Stout Farm. Look out for the footpath on your right above an earthwork causeway and several large stone walls that are a part of the mediaeval area. With the earthwork behind you will find the two stiles above Williambeer Farm. Bare left with the lane and then next right to lead you past the milk churns at Hoemoor Farm, until you come to Knackers Hole Lane. Bare left to bring you onto the Otterford /Churchinford Road and then right half a mile to home.

" What kind of a future will there be here for these young people"?

"It is pretty certain that this will be the only kind of tractor that this young man will ever drive on the land".

A Hidden Mediaeval Village

It is part of the character of the Blackdown Hills not to reveal their secrets too easily. Our next visit is to a hidden valley site where great stone walls up to 9 ft. thick and of the same in height, protect the foundations of an ancient village. Could this be the remains of the mythological **'City at Churchstanton'?** Certainly the village once covered some 40 acres and that is no understatement!

*We exit **Churchinford** towards **Upottery.** After half a mile we take the first lane left and turn right, down over the hill at a fork. This leads you through lovely Lower Luxton farm and past the Milk Churns and Self Catering at **Hoemoor Farm**. You cross the Otter River and come to a 'T' Junction after a short distance. Bear Left to **Williambeer Farm** and the stile leading you to the ancient village site is on your right. Car parking is a problem here, so ask the farmer where is best!*

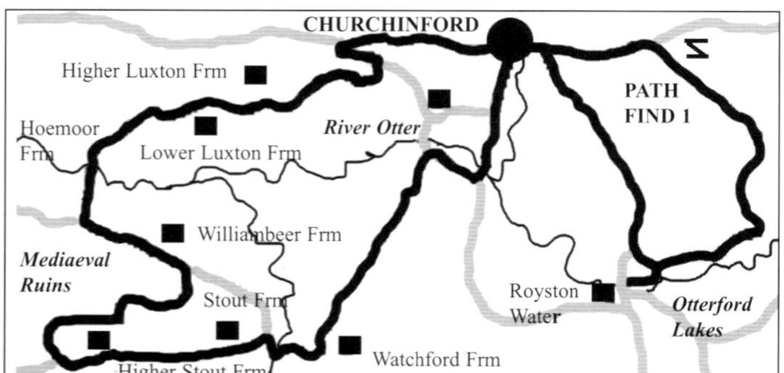

The Public pathway from Williambeer Farm takes us through two stiles where we follow the uphill hedge on our right. The terrain breaks right with the walls and village below us and an earthwork above. Some of the walls here are 9 feet high, far beyond the needs of keeping stock, their width providing high flat platforms for defence and an efficient infrastructure for getting from one place to another over the boggy terrain.

Either side of these structures, piles of large stones suggest a maze of buildings leading from a central enclosure up to a defensive earthwork and defendable causeway through Nothams Farm.

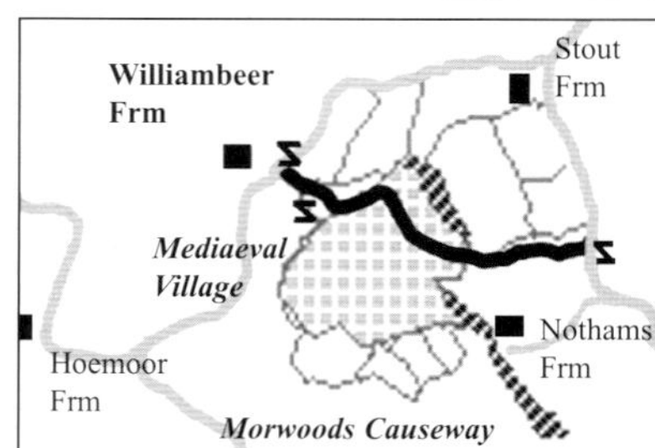

UPOTTERY AND RAWRIDGE

We resume our journey to return from Williambeer Farm, keeping the enclave of delightful farm buildings on our right. We keep straight on through Twistgates and up to Rookery Farm, where we take the right fork and make a right again, to follow the road through Phillishayes. Another right turn, will lead us past the fine village hall and the 'unnerving slope' of the cricket pitch, into ***Upottery***. That **Upottery** was a place of some importance is immediately reflected in the architecture. What exists today is a far cry from the huddle of Saxon houses presided over by Alric the Priest, during King Harold's reign. The Church is recently restored with a magnificent vicarage, whose meadow ponds were a battle ground for **Frederick Janes** (author of Janes Fighting Ships) and his brothers, as they fought regular sea battles with models and real gunpowder. Within the Church there is the remains of Norman corbel table and a 13th. century piscina (Washing basin for the vessels of the sacrament).

Upottery Vicarage

East Devon Hunt at The Sidmouth Arms : Photo Pete Rigler.

Central to the village is the **'Sidmouth Arms'**, another favourite Blackdown hostelry for great food and good cheer. This Inn is named after the son of the 19th. century owner of Upottery Manor Dr. John Addington. **Henry Addington** became First Viscount of Sidmouth and served as **Prime Minister** from 1801 to 1804. Opposite The Sidmouth Arms is the gatehouse to the Manor belonging to the **Cheney** Family in the 13th. century. At one time, Henry 2nd. is supposed to have appropriated Rawridge Manor as an income for the Church in exchange for £100. However, the new owners leased it back to Sir William Cheney, for a rent of a pound of beeswax to be paid annually at Michaelmas. "Methinks t'was a fine arrangement!"

The cricket ground here is built into the hillside and even the slightest edge off the bat to the down side can run for four or even six. It is a game which survives well in the Blackdowns, with the continuing support of pubs and those ever resourceful wives, making the teas. *We continue on our exploration by leaving the Upottery Church lynch gate on our left, to follow the Otter River and the valley that widens out rapidly, as we approach the neighbouring hamlet of* ***Rawridge***.

Monkton and Beacon

If you like to exercise your swing, the **Otter Valley Golf Centre** provides 9 practice holes and lessons to improve your handicap. This is to be found just up on your left before entering **Rawridge**. The village has a post office shop and is on the regular route for the little red post bus, which also calls at Combe Raleigh, Dunkeswell, Luppitt, Smeatharpe, Upottery, Monkton and Honiton. There are some pretty homes here, overlooking the River Otter towards Mohuns Ottery.

A 4 mile walk from the south end of the village can be found by crossing the river Otter through Spurtham Farm and onto the ***Hartridge Walk*** *(Page 71). This takes you across the top of Hartridge Common by the track that cuts across to the Hamlet of Beacon.*

On leaving Rawridge, a mile will bring us to an intersection with the A303, where we bare right onto the southbound lane to the roadside Village of Monkton. Perhaps this an ideal moment for a little refreshment at **The Monkton Arms** and it is from here is best explored the 19th. century church of **St. Mary Magdalene**. Within, are links with Mohuns Ottery, confirmed by a vault inscribed to Thomas Southcote, who farmed the Ottery during the latter part of the 1600's.

Field patterns between Rawridge and Monkton

Devon Longhouse and enclosed yard Beacon.

Otters made 'Good hunting sport' with hounds until recently along these river banks, in the knowledge that these gay and playful riverside creatures could decimate fish populations, if not culled. Seemingly otters were bred in captivity at Mohuns for the qualities of their pelts. Perhaps in the 18th. century these were superseded by the importing of American beaver pelts, so fashionable in the manufacture of top hats and muffs. Whatever the reason for the decline, Mohuns Ottery looks a grey and forbidding building in comparison to the spirit of the wonderful creatures, to which it owes its name.

As we continue through Monkton village we look for a turning off the A303 to your right to lead you into the hamlet of ***Beacon*** *on turning right at the first 'T' Junction.*

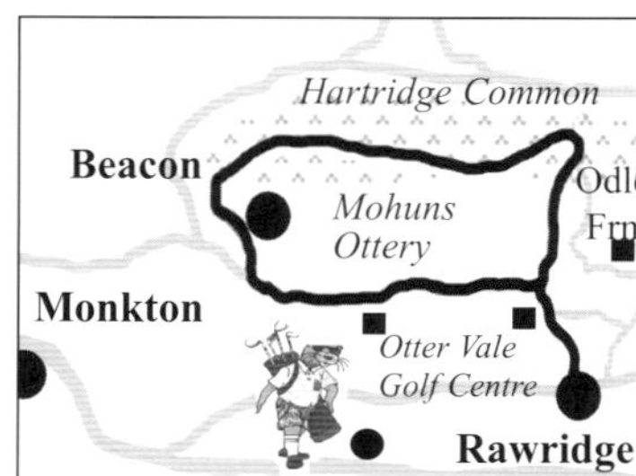

DUMPDON HILL

When looking West from **Beacon** we see how nature has supplied the natural resource for man to make a fortification. The geological make up of the 261 meter high Dumpdon Hill has resisted the forces of water of the river Otter and it's tributaries, to become shaped like a natural Sphinx against the skyline.

An inexorably warning perhaps to all those approaching the Blackdowns to have a special care, if they come with ill intent. The present archaeology suggests that **Dumpdon** was an iron age fort with a raised bank at its crown. Yet it may have been used earlier. The pattern of fields on the slopes around Dumpdon's N/W base are small, irregular and probably Saxon in origin. A forest of bracken surrounds the earthwork, to turn a rich golden brown, in Autumn.

We approach Dumpdon Hill from ***Beacon*** *by following the lane between the two farms, that were once were the nucleus of the hamlet. One still a vibrant working farm, the other a delightful home under thatch. We keep* ***left*** *at the signpost to* ***Wick.*** *After a half mile journey through the wooded lane, we find the small* ***National Trust*** *car park to* ***Dumpdon Hill Fort****.*

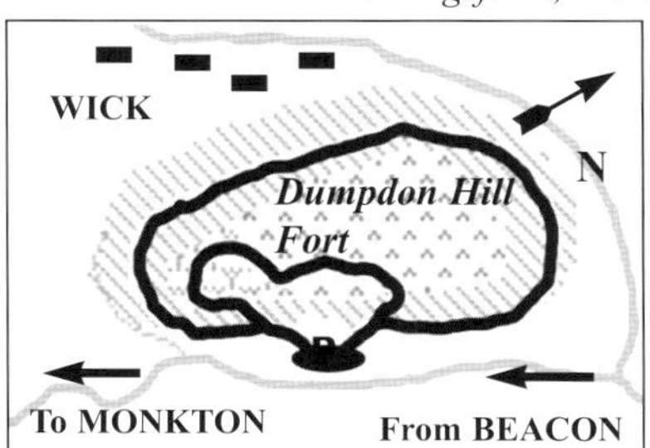

The pathway leading from here takes you completely around the base of the Fort.

For those who don't mind a steep climb, a track upwards leads you directly into the trees, where hints of the original single ditched earthworks can be made out in the meadow grass at the top. Fine panoramic views are to be had of the Blackdowns from every angle! To the West the sun may shine off the growing houses at **Jackson's & Sons Ltd**, who grow hundreds of thousands of those early spring plant plugs, for nurseries throughout the South West.

A right turn from the car park leads us down the narrow lane back to the Honiton /Dunkeswell road. Take a left turn at the 'T' junction to bring you home to Honiton and the end of Route 4.

Photo courtesy F. J. Jackson & Son

AXMINSTER was a town of importance long before the advent of the industrial revolution and the development of the large factory complex, who's name brand for the high quality carpets would become famous World wide. Also, it was in the valley of the Axe a battle took place, that was to shape the concept of monarchy for the whole of England. The grandson of King Alfred, (He who burnt the cakes) fought the battle of Brunaburgh, to establish himself as Athelstan King of all England near here in the mid 8th. century. This Southern section of the Blackdowns are perhaps the most spectacular in that so little has been spoilt here and so few people have discovered them.

Circular
Route 5
The South from Axminster

An Endless Rolling Sea of Green

In saving our route into the Blackdowns from Axminster to the last, we are in danger of being accused of leaving the best to the end. For our journey through the Southern part of the AONB is destined to take us through an endless roller coaster ride of virgin rare and unspoilt English countryside. A great continuum of rolling hills and valleys, where the traveller is successively lost and found, as a small ship might be, amongst great friendly mid-ocean waves. The lush fields and high hedgerows are home to an abundance of plant species and wild creatures. A haven where the only indulgences of mankind are clusters of cottages and farmsteads. Yet, in this place even they seem to grow out of the mother earth, as of their own accord.

Axminster like all the other towns which serve the Blackdowns is a hive of activity, with a modern industrial estate, several small factories, a shopping centre and a livestock market which pre-dates the 700 year old tower of the **Church of St. Mary the Virgin.** A heritage fashioned in wool led to the famous carpet weaving at Axminster, the factory dating from 1755. Blackdown fleeces were woven into the fine thick pile by the tiny hands and cruelty of child labour, where so great was the challenge in finishing a carpet, that a bell would be rung at St Marys in celebration, each time a carpet received the final stitch!

We leave Axminster from the centre of the town and take the road North, opposite the 18th. century coaching inn of ***The George Hotel.*** *This leads us down over the railway tracks to the river Axe, signed to the village of* ***Membury****. After three quarters of a mile we take the right fork in the road up through the steep escarpments of Green Down.* The highest point of which is the iron age fort and Roman encampment of **Membury Castle Fort**, some 3 miles out of Axminster. You may be surprised by a painted road sign directing any horses on the road to turn right into High Lea Farm. This part of the Blackdowns is equine heaven and has an abundance of bridle ways, making the area excellent hacking and hunting country.

MEMBURY FORT

Finding **Membury Castle** is not as easy as one might assume. The village is deep in the valley floor on your left. When the church tower of **St John the Baptist** comes in sight, start looking out for the public pathway on your right to the ancient monument. A footpath also leads up from the village to a slight widening in the road, where there is just about room to park a vehicle without causing a severe obstruction, if it is left tight into the hedge! Membury is one of the few major ancient sites in the Blackdowns not to be served with some form of parking nearby. One designated footpath passes around the southern end, another takes you to the monument from the Churchill Road. The site is not posted against trespass, although it was surrounded by a dangerous electric fence, when we last walked there. The effort of climbing the steep hillside will be rewarded with the experience of visiting a very complete defensive enclosure, that once dominated the valleys between the Yarty and the Roman Fosse Way (A358). The raised banks that make up the defenses are underpinned with stone and there is evidence to suggest a very sophisticated fort existed here.

Tree roots cling to the ancient Stone Walls at Membury

Nothing is plain Black and White at Membury

It is possible that Membury was so secure, the Romans were able to use the fort as a sort of 'Butlins' and 'R&R' for troops recovering from the harsh posting that Britain must have been. This idea might also be based on evidence that **King Athelstane** may have sent his battle worn troops here for convalescence after defeating the Danes. Perhaps after the battle of **Brunneburg** in 937. The ‘Mem’ could be a derivative of 'Maim' as in Maimburgh. Nearby at Membury Court are the remains of a Roman Villa which was excavated just before the Great War and an amphora of the Roman period but of Turkish origin, was found in a cottage garden in the village. Legend fervours legend at Membury fort but what is certain is that it should respected as a place of ancient origins and one to be preserved.

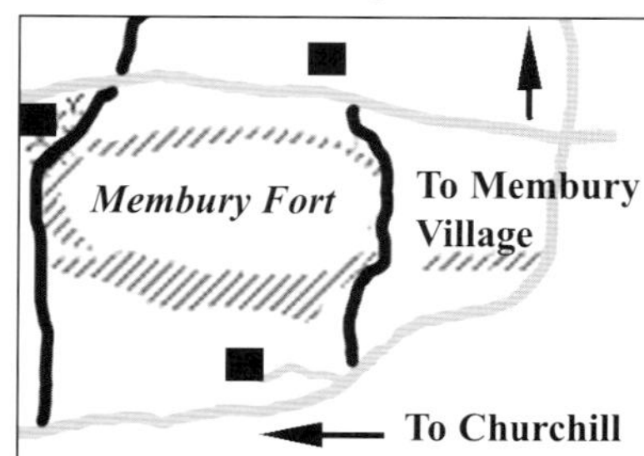

MEMBURY

Membury must be one of our favourite Villages on the Blackdowns despite the nearest pub, **The Longbridge Inn** is 2 very long miles away down a maze of very 'Pixie-related' lanes. Coming down the hill from the fort you see the cluster of cottages and an attendant chestnut tree, to immediately make you feel welcome, even if you haven't ever played the game of 'conkers - "Come on mate I've got twenty two'er!"-

"Naah - no way - likely its a baker!" A perfectly proportioned white wooden tower houses the bell to toll the lessons of the School House. This nestles in the shadows of the 14th. century tower of the Church of **St. John the Baptist.** The tower is guarded by 4 grotesque gargoyles, known as the 'Hunky Punks'. At the North end near the 'Conker tree' is the friendliest of **Village Post Office Shops** selling nearly everything that you would wish for. The wine, farm fresh pork and the determination of the owners Pauline and Keith Jacobs to provide a village service beyond all others, won this little shop, **The Virgin Cola Customer Care Challenge,** for the whole of the UK" in 1998. Behind the 200 year old tree is the village playing field, where the sounds of leather, willow and children's voices echo down the vale to the miniature church built by 13 year old John Beasley in 1826.

*We travel down the narrow valley road through the village, to the **Manorial Mill at Rock**.* Here, you can buy fresh and smoked fish and upon request you can feed the trout in the ponds that are open to the public. Perhaps it is the music of the cheerful little stream, as it passes through the flower drenched gardens along the road, which sets the harmony of life here. The effect is, that the people still make the time and have the will to pass the time of day with each other.

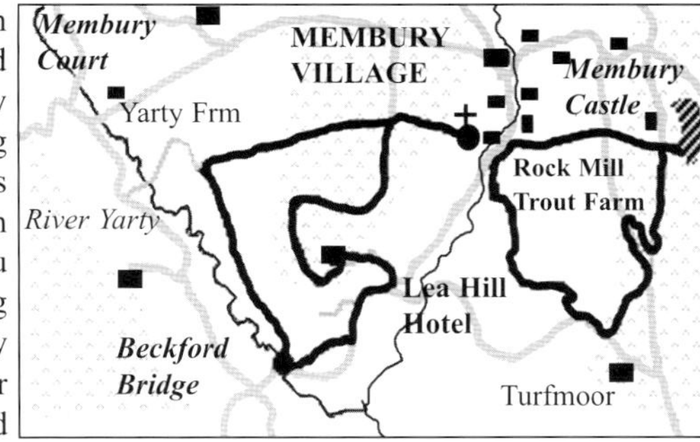

Here you can expect a wave and a "Hi!" for any strangers passing by. So infectious is this place with goodwill, you can't help giving yourself that very same chance for acquaintance and invite the opportunity for friendship with those who live here.

The Ancient name for Membury was Maenborg. (A secure and fortified place). The Manor was called Maaberia at Doomsday. **Pound House** is now a **working pottery**, where in the studio, a prehistoric burial urn was found in a workshop alcove. The house lies directly below the Church and we may suppose that here was built a Christian Church on a holy site of the 'Olden Druid' ways. The village would have been home to many ancient crafts. Bakers, wheelwrights, cobblers, carpenters and blacksmiths. Apple cheeses on old wooden presses are still assembled to produce that beautiful golden Devon cider. Go into the village shop and buy the wonderfully illustrated parish map designed by the villagers. The people here are very proud of Membury. There are circular walks up to Membury Fort and east to the River Yarty to the medieval pack horse bridge at Beckford and back.

Lea Hill, Beckford and the Yarty

We leave Membury with the pottery to our right to follow the little brook past **Rock Mill Trout Farm.** The road takes us up the side of Lea Hill. A driveway on our right takes us to the mediaeval farmhouse that was once the property of the **Quaker John Smith**, who was tried at 'The Bloody Assizes. The house and barns have been lovingly restored to offer the tranquillity of **Lea Hill Country House Hotel**, where the finest of comfort and cuisine is found. Goyle Acre Lane is an easy track from the hotel, along which is a Quaker Burial Ground. Just below the property there was a 'Friends Meeting House'. The geographical position of which to Whitehall Woods, gave the opportunity for a safe refuge for the friends, from religious persecutors.

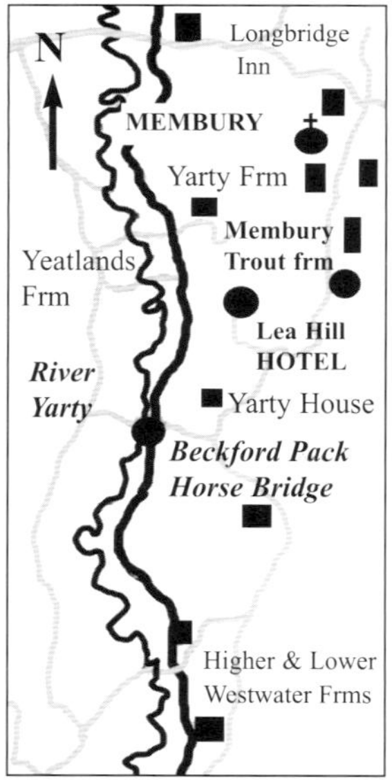

Lea Hill Hotel

Beckford Bridge

History has often touched this area but never ravaged it. **Monmouth** visited Membury Fort on his way to defeat at **Sedgemoor** and **Sir Shilston Calmady** was killed at **Ford House** during the Civil War.

We turn right from Lea Hill into the lane for a quarter of a mile, to the Yarty bottoms, where we come to the delightful symmetry of the ancient ***Pack Horse Bridge at Beckford***. It is the finest example of its kind in this part of the Westcountry. From here we are able to walk the riverbanks of the Yarty for almost two miles, both North and south. The bridge lies midway between the Longbridge Arms to the North and Lower West Water Farm to the South.

Dalwood and Danes Hill

Horner Hill

*We cross the Yarty at **Beckford Bridge** and turn left along the valley lane to parallel the meandering River Yarty. The valley slowly opens out into a wide flood plain just below Axminster. We travel the lane for a mile to take the first turning right, which lead us past Dulcis Farm to 'Danes Hill'.*

This is the first of three great Hills which overlook the village of **Dalwood**. **Horner Hill** is the highest at 221 meters and the slightly lower Beacon Hill is at 218 meters.

Any of these very defendable hills would have been a good place to set up the shield lines and sharp stakes against an invading army. What is not known, is if there were any important battle here.

*To find Dalwood from the side of **Danes Hill**, we bare left at the crossway and left again to bring us into the cluster of chocolate box cottages surrounding the* **Norman Tower of St. Peter's Church.**

February fills the Corrie Brook at Dalwood

The Tuckers Arms, Dalwood

Central to this pretty village is **The Tuckers Arms**. A traditional pub, which perhaps has been most successful in surviving brewery modernisations, here on the Hills. You feel as if the earthy locals of many centuries past, might suddenly leap out of the walls and tell of times both good and bad, which have been had within this cheery place. Flagstone floors are underfoot and original oak partitions make for a series of nooky corners to enjoy the excellent food and cellar found here - and its good value too! The building was used as a hunting lodge by the **Dukes of Beaulieu**. 14th. century parts of the pub remain today standing on land given by **William the Conqueror** himself. Our favourite perch is by the gloriously cluttered 16th. century inglenook.

Dalwood Walks and Stockland Castles

To know the countryside surrounding Dalwood, is to have walked it. There is a short walk straight up the escarpment to the top of Danes Hill to return by the footpath found near the cottage at its Southern End. This walk can be extended to Beckford. There is also a 3 mile walk starting behind the 15th. century Church of St. Peters to lead up through Hawley Bottoms. This comes out at Coombes Head Farm, where you can return through the rich wild forestry by a bridleway. Look out for Mickey Mouse in topiary. Fancy takes us on a 'Silly Day', that the character has accidentally slipped out of children's broadcasting, from the Stockland TV Transmitter, a mile of so West of the village.

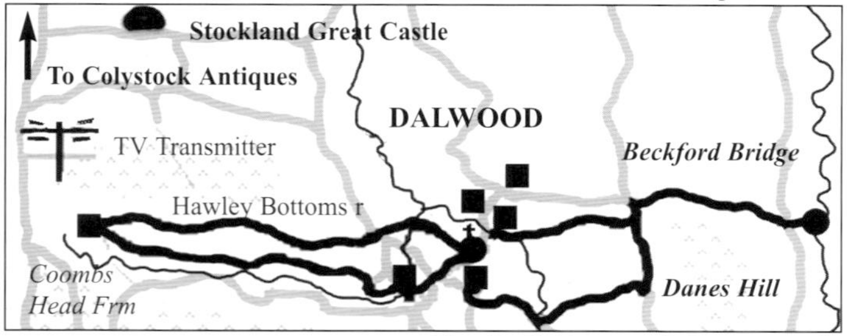

Ancient lane to Little Stockland Castle

The Bell Tower of **St Peters** is only some 45 feet high with an exterior staircase. The short piers supporting the Beer stone arcade between the naive and the aisle are thought to have been worked in the 12th. century. In competition, a mile south of the village is the **Loughwood Meeting House**, amongst the oldest Baptist buildings in the country, being completed in 1643. The building is part of Loughwood farm, now owned by the National Trust.

Outer bank of Little Stockland Castle

To leave Dalwood we aim East towards the TV transmitter. At the intersection we bare right, leaving the transmitter on our right. At the second intersection, if we take the left, we can make a short detour to the walled Church of ***St Michael at Cotleigh.*** *Go straight on for a mile if you wish to savour the antique and reproduction furnishings at* ***Colystock*** *Showrooms.* To continue our journey, we travel a half mile on the straight road and then bare right to find the half circle of deciduous woodland on our left, (300 meters). This is all that is left of **Great Stockland Castle**. View it from the roadside iron gates. Through the trees you can see what is left of stone walls and a steep ditch. Little Stockland Castle, a mile away, is more accessible by a track, with its down hill wall raised some 16 ft. in height as part of a long line of defensive forts across the hills.

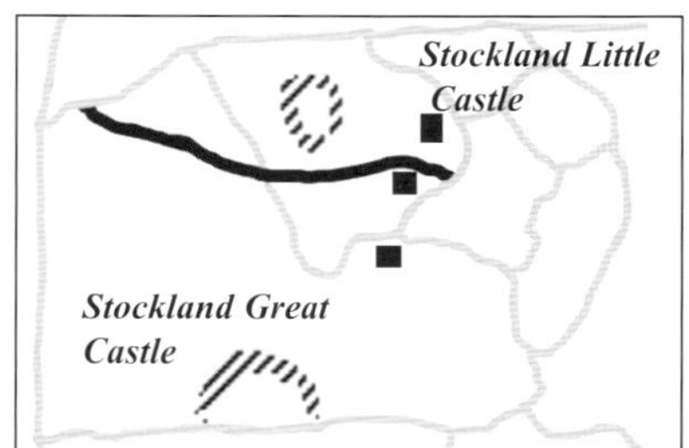

STOCKLAND

There is every chance of becoming lost in **Shore Bottoms.** There are no less than ten lanes entering or exiting this one square mile of Blackdown domain. *However, there is a solution. at the Little Castle. Put your back to the TV transmitter and head East and you will eventually be sign posted to the Village of Stockland.*

Stockland is a very, 'Altogether Community'. A great variety of events go on throughout the year, thanks to a spacious village hall set amidst several acres of playing fields. The capping pride of village organisation is the annual **Bank Holiday May Fair**, which attracts thousands of people from all over the area. This is a true joy of a country event with folk determined to continue the tradition, ever since Henry 3rd gave Stockland the right to hold fairings, in 1252. A signed charter affirming this, hangs in the Church of St Michael and All Saints. Literally 1000's of stone and iron age artifacts have been found in the area to include stone picks, axes and 10,000 year old microliths. (Flint arrow heads).

The Village council has become 'Lord of the Manor', so that it can protect the **Turbaries.** (Common land with the right for commoners to dig turf or peat for fuel). Turbaries are under threat from land improvement and the particular environment they provide is very rare in the Devonshire parishes. The 14 /15th. century tower of **St Michaels** is in a perfect and secluded setting, standing probably on an original pagan site. It is surrounded by a wealth of thatched cottages, a primary school and a very successful traditional public house with restaurant.

The **Kings Arms Inn**. is perhaps so named, because of the loyalty of 3 soldiers from the parish to Charles 2nd. who were rewarded with a pension of 40 shillings in 1663. The Inn is a must for replenishment, with a fine dining room and quality accommodation within its ancient walls. The pub is a rarity where that all so essential balance between quality catering and the needs of the locals, has been caringly maintained.

We leave uphill from the village with our backs to the Church, as if on route to Yarcombe. After a half mile the road forks and we take the right to bring us to the 18th. century Long Bridge. This part of the Blackdowns used to be Dorset in the middle 1800's. On the bridge, as on another in the village, is a very determined notice, warning over exuberant wagon and coach drivers, that if they were to damage the structure, upon conviction they may be transported for life! A brief history of the parish is available, recorded

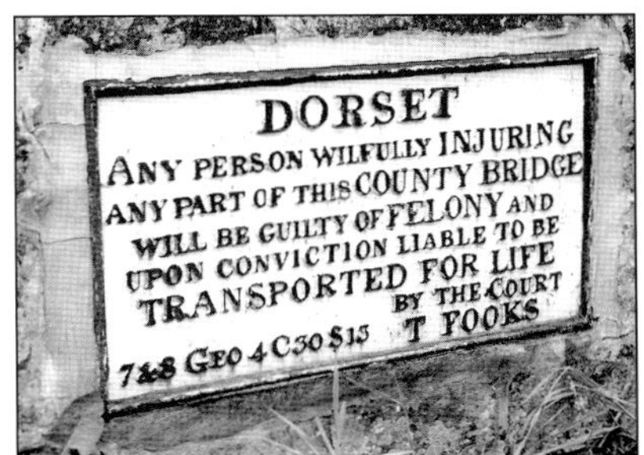

Two Blackdown Pioneers

The Longbridge Inn

The Longbridge Inn remained decorated as a 1950's time warp, until recently. It has just been refurbished with stone floors and timbers, returned to a traditional country Inn. A wood fire can be found on cold days in the original inglenook. On a fine day it makes for an excellent base, from which to discover the Yarty. The pub is famous for it's double laned Skittles Alley and the Summer competition can leave a mountain of empty barrels to be seen for miles in all directions.

Up over the hill from the Inn, the next lane right, will bring you to **Land Farm.** Here is the birth place in 1795, of **Thomas Wakley**, the medical and social reformer who was the founding editor of the oldest still in print magazine, **The Lancet.**

To continue on route No.5, we head East up the hill leaving the Longbridge on our left and onto the top of ***Bewley Down****. We follow this for two miles, until the road forks. The right fork leading to* ***Wambrook****, the left towards the* ***Ferne Animal Sanctuary.*** If we look over the large arable fields to our right, it is from here that the Victorian inventor **Mr. John Stringfellow,** attempted to fly a variety of steam powered, unmanned flying machines fuelled with methylated spirits, as early as 1846.

Bewley Down

Stringfellow's work was recognised only when he exhibited his flying machine at the Crystal Palace in 1868. It would have made for a very strange sight for those Blackdown farm workers toiling in the fields, as horse and dray brought the strange, weird creations through the narrow lanes from Mr. Stringfellow's able mind, to their testing grounds on the high ground of the Blackdown plain. We turn left onto the road that leads us to the **Ferne Animal Sanctuary.** The 51 acres over looking the beautiful Yarty Valley, now offer a safe home to some 300 animals. Moreover, visitors are encouraged to enjoy their company in the quiet sanctity of this place. There is a **tea room** and you may picnic in the grounds, with a nature trail to discover. Ferne is supported solely by public donations. Dogs and cats are re-homed within a 30 mile radius. Ferne's precepts are to instruct in humane education; to open the minds of children and adults to see that animals are indeed part of God's creation and deserve the same respect, compassion and justice, as do our fellow humans.

WAMBROOK

We continue past the ***Ferne Animal Sanctuary*** *to look out for the 'Red Sign Post' and turn right, past* ***Higher Wambrook Farm.*** The house and buildings are quite grand with extended eaves and replica Norman arched doorways. In the middle of the yard is a quaint Chapel like granary. Inside is the original paymasters desk, when the 300 acre farm would have employed up to a dozen men during the Victorian era.

When I visited **Wambrook** during the mid-week, I was enthralled to find that over 200 locals had filled the little Church of St Mary's, to pay their respects to one who had passed away from this small community. I felt that this gathering was just as much a protest against change, as it was reverent in mourning a friend, who's memory was written indelibly into the values of the past. Wambrook seems a place determined to resist as best it can the break down of the established country way of life. From **The Cotley Arms** there are seemingly endless footpaths and quiet lanes from which to explore the exquisite countryside.

A good circular walk, (2 miles) is to start from the track that runs past the pub. Take the left fork towards the Church. At the Church, cross the lane and take the footpath on your left. This will take you up the hill to Lancing Farm. Turn right along the lane and look out right for the footpath to Higher Wambrook and down the lane to home.

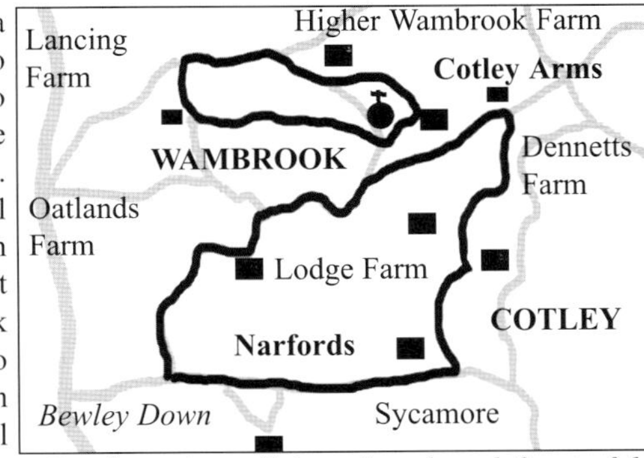

Wambrook is a special place to stay if you wish to be far from the madding crowd. There are several B & B's. You can stay on farms at Higher Wambrook and Weston, or go back to school in the old school house at Woodview. *Our favourite walk here, is to bear left out of the Cotley Arms car park, after a good lunch and head up the hill to Dennetts Farm. Just opposite is a track which develops into a footpath. This takes you between Cotley and Lodge Farm to Narford. Bear right up the long, fairly steep incline of the tarmac road to take you up onto Bewley Down. Near the top, look out for the track which leads right, back down to Oatlands Farm, through the forestry and right back to Wambrook Village and home.*

The Cotley Arms at Wambrook has become renowned for the high quality food that is served here. Especially, that all so traditional roast luncheon. on the weekend. Please book early to avoid disappointment. In addition, the tranquil garden is a delight on a fine day, as are the superb prawn sandwiches.

Through Holy City to Chardstock

We leave Wambrook with the Cotley Arms on our right, up the hill and onto Bewley Down. We bear left and follow the hill top road for 2 miles until the sign to **Holy City**. Take the left and a mile East of this hamlet

through the lanes is the stone built village of **Chardstock.** Here is a place with a character achieved through an altogether civilised piece of planning. On climbing up past the miniature footbridge, we are invited to enter the centre by a generously wide street serving the well founded **St Andrews Church**, vicarage and primary school. Behind that is the 14th. century Manor House of Chardstock Court, which once was owned by the **Bishop of Salisbury**. The village is graced with both a pub and a hotel. **The George Inn** and the **The George Hotel**, until recently the The Tytherleigh Cot. The latter offers country hotel accommodations under thatch, graced with a fine restaurant. The George Inn is another virtually unspoilt Blackdown hostelry serving a great selection of ales and food. It has a scrolled wooden screen from a 12th. century manor house, reputed to have more value than the freehold of the pub itself.

St Andrews Church was renovated and like many of its kind, much of

the original was lost in the 1800's. However, several of the now redundant, devil like gargoyles are now at ground level and therefore, better to scrutinise. Each very much weather worn from being once perched high up on the Norman tower.

As we exit by the way we came and turn South at the top of Bewley Down towards the A358, we come to the end of this journey through the Blackdowns. On descending the high escarpments we almost seem to need that shiny Airstream trailer from Mission Control to ease our transition from the tranquillity of these beautiful landscapes, into whatever lies beyond. Despite this, we hope that within these few finished, yet incomplete pages, to have conveyed some insights into what is the real nature of the Blackdowns at the turn of this millennium. In truth we have only turned over but a few of the stones that exist in this place and we assure you there is ample room left for surprise and intrigue to be found here, when exploring these hidden hills and valleys for yourselves. *M.D.B.*

COMMUNITY INFORMATION

Emergency Numbers:

FIRE - 999 - POLICE - 999 - AMBULANCE - 999 -

Avon & Somerset Constabulary - 01275 818181
Devon & Cornwall Constabulary - 01392 52101
Crime stoppers - 0800 555 111

Electricity - 01823 335258 | Gas - 0345 222999
Water Supply - 0345 300600 | National Rivers Authority - 0345 078378

Doctors

The Blackdown Practice, Station Road, Hemyock. - 01823 680206
The Blackdown Practice, Churchinford. - 01823 601221
The Blackdown Practice, Culme Way, Dunkeswell. - 01404 891861
The Surgery, St. Thomas Court, Church Street, Axminster. - 01297 32126

Veterinary Practices

Acorn Clinic, Little Fosgrove, Blagdon Hill. - 01823 421554
J.C. Equine Services, Orchard Court, West Buckland, Wellington - 01823 661448
Lee and Brain, Fancy Lane, Dunkeswell. - 01404 42750
Lewis-Jones Ass, 29A, Station Road, Hemyock. - 01823 681067
Coombefield Vet Hospital, Coombe Ln, Axminster. - 01297 32156
The Vale Group, 7, Fore Street, Uffculme. - 01884 841317

Weather Information

Weathercall - Somerset - 0891 50505 - Devon - 0891 50504 South West - 0891 505358
Marinecall - Mid Channel/Solent - 0891 505357 - Bristol Channel - 0891 505359

Important Local Initiatives

THE BLACKDOWN HILL PROJECT: - Contact David Dixon.
White House Cottage, Stockland, Devon. EX14 9DS - Tel. 01404 881733.
JOINT ADVISORY COMMISSION - Chair. Chris Robinson - Tel. 01823 421667.
BRITISH TRUST FOR CONSERVATION VOLUNTEERS
Devon Office, The Arts Centre, Gandy Street, Exeter. - 401392 424547
SOUTH WEST ARTS - Judith Higginbottom - Bristol - 0117 927 3226
Cats Protection League - Honiton - 01404 45241

THE BLACKDOWN SUPPORT GROUP. - Contact Brian Simpson.
Volunteers giving extra help in the community, to that already provided by the Doctors, Nurses, Health Visitors & Physiotherapists, Social Workers etc.
The Surgery, Station Rd. Hemyock, Devon. EX15 3SF -Tel. 01823 681036.

Libraries

Axminster - South Street. - 01297 32693 : Cullompton - 2 Exeter Hill. - 01884 33628
Honiton - 48 New Street. - 01404 42818 : Uffculme - 8 Ashley Road. - 01884 840522
Chard - Boden Street - 01460 63321 : Priorswood Library - 01823 272050
Taunton - Main & Local History Library Paul St.- 01823 336334
Wellington - 16, Fore Street - 01823 662635

Museums

Allhallows Museum, High Steet, Honiton. - 01404 44966.
Coldhabour Working Wool Museum, Uffculme. - 01884 840960.
Dunkeswell Memorial Museum, Dunkeswell Airfield. - 01404 891943.
Sheppys Cider Farm & Museum, Bradford on Tone. - 01823 461233.
Chard 'Stringfellow' and Agricultural Museum, Chard. - 01460 67463.
Wellington Museum, The Squirrel, Wellington. - 01823 664747.

Local News Papers, TV and Radio Stations.

Newscom Somerset Gazette Series - 01823 365151 : Taunton Times - 01823 251132
Chard and Ilminster News - 01460 633442 : Express & Echo - 01392 442211
Western Morning News - 01392 254267 : Mid Devon Express and Star - 01884 255977
Mid Devon Gazette - 01884 252725 : Sidmouth Herald - 01395 515192
: Wellington Weekly News - 01823 662439
HTV West - 01823 270293 : BBC TV Bristol - 0117 9732211
Westcountry TV - 01823 499400 : BBC TV Plymouth - 01752 229201
Gemini Radio - 01392 444444 : BBC Somerset Sound - 01823 251641
Orchard FM - 01823 338448 : BBC Radio Devon - 01392 215651

SPORTS ASSOCIATIONS AND CLUBS

Ramblers Association : - Devon - 01404 884635 Somerset - 01823 323147
British Field Sports Society - Mr. Mal Trharne - 01278 671818
National Rifle Association - Mr. R Mason. Taunton - 01823 42479
Blackdown Hedging Association - Mr. D. Palmer - 01823 680467
Gatchell House Squash Country Club - Trull, Taunton - 01823 333261
Wellington Squash Club - Coranas Ln, Wellington - 01823 656232
Cresta Sports Centre - Chard - 01460 30231 : **Wellington Sports Centre** - 01823 663010
Taunton Swimming Pool - 0140 254106 : **Culm Valley Sports Centre** - 01884 32853
Axminster Valley Sports Centre - 01297 35235 : Honiton Sports Centre - 01404 42325.
Blackdown Young Farmers Clubs : Culm Valley : Yarcombe : Honiton : Cullompton : Sid & Otter Vale : Axminster : All information through Central office - 01392 272189.

Community Information & Transport

TOURIST INFORMATION CENTRES

Axminster Old Court House, Church St.. Axminster. - 01297 34386
Honiton - Dowell St. East Car Park, Honiton. - 01404 43716
Chard - The Guild Hall, Fore Street, Chard. - 01460 67463
Taunton - The Library, Paul St. Taunton. - 01823 336334
Wellington - 28, Fore Street, Wellington. - 01823 664747
Willand Motorway Services. Junction 27. - 01884 821242

VILLAGE INFORMATION POINTS

Blagdon Hill Post Office and Stores, TA3 7SG. Tel: 01823 421448
Buckland St.Mary Post Office ,Chard,TA203SJ. Tel: 01460 234225
Combe St Nicholas Post office. Tel: 01460 62106
Hemyock Post Office and Stores Tel: 01823 680259
West Buckland Post Office, Taunton, TA21 91U. Tel: 01823 667997
Stopgate Service Station. A303. Tel: 01404 861 214/376

TRAVEL

British Rail Enquiries: Tel: 01392 433551
British Rail - Taunton Station Tel: 01823 283444
Southern National Ltd., The Bus Station, Taunton Tel: 01823 272033
Devon Bus Enquiries Tel: 01392 382800
National Express Coaches Tel: 01392 215454
The Post Bus, The Sorting Office, High St., Honiton. Tel: 01404 42001
Honiton & District Ring & Ride for the disabled or elderly Tel: 01404 46529
Taunton Dean Community Transport for the disabled or elderly Tel: 01823 331266
Transport for the disabled in Somerset, Mr. J. Chaimers Tel: 01823 255695
Transport for the disabled in Somerset, (Yeovil) Tel: 01935 75914

COACH HIRE

Johnny Batton, Monkton Tel: 01404 42142
Redwoods Travel, Hemyock. Tel: 01823 680288
R.A. Goodman, Mini Bus Hire, Gorse Cottage, Culmhead. Tel: 01823 421795
Sewards Coaches, Glendale, Dalwood, Axminster. Tel: 01404 881343
Honiton Mini Coaches, 50, Market Way, Honiton. Tel: 01404 44137

BICYCLE HIRE

Cycle (Honiton), Lanson House, King Street, Honiton. Tel: 01404 47211
Kings Cycles, 7, Cornhill, Wellington, Som. Tel: 01823 662260

TAXIS

Alpha Cars, 1, Dumpdon View, Monkton. Tel: 01404 41622
AtoB Cabs,76, Highland Terrace,Uffculme.Devon Tel: 01884 840853

VILLAGE COMMUNITY INFORMATION

Compiled by The Blackdown Practice Patients' Participation Group with additions by Local Parish Councils.

ALL SAINTS:

All Saints Primary School - Mrs. Christine Hollidge - Head teacher 01297 32761
Pre-School-Lucy Herod-01297 35707 : Mother/Toddler Group- Sue Brown 01460 221475
Cricket Club - Cliff Farmer 01460 221178 : Archery Club Ray Prior 01460 221410
Antiquarian Society - John Dangerfield 01297 33326
Mothers Union - J. Wellington 01460 221228 : Scouts/Cubs - Mr.W. Forsey 01297 32674
Girl Guides / Brownies - J. Verplancke 01297 32768 :
Recorded Music Soc - C Ross 01297 33300 : Pantomime Soc - J. Ross 01297 333000
Parish Letter - Sue Brown 01460 221475 : Women's Institute - L. Doman 01297 34269
All Saints Parish Church - Rev Ruth Waring 01460 220005
Methodist chapel - Rev Martin Bailey 01460 63289
Village Fete - July - Carole Baulch - 01297 32171 : School May Fayre - 01297 - 32761
W.I. Carol Concert (Dec) & Flower Show (Sept) - 01297 34269

AWLISCOMBE:

Awliscombe Parish Council - Clerk - Mrs E Gillingham - 01404 43551
Primary School - 01404 42031 : Nursery Group - Mrs E. Street - 01404 41854
Awliscombe Parish Church - Rev G. Hutchins - The Vicarage - 01404 42983
Parish News - Mrs Abbott - 01404 42361 : Toddler Group - Mrs K. Smith 01404 45729
W. I - Mrs Chandler 01404 44404 : Parish Hall - Mrs Summers - 01404 41703
Young Wives - Mrs A. Quick - 01404 841207 : Over 60's Mrs R. Sprigg - 01404 43814
Friday Youth Club (A Christian Organisation) Mrs P. Edwards - 01404 43729
Ex Servicemen and Womens Association - Mr. R. Sprigg - 01404 43814

VILLAGE COMMUNITY INFORMATION

Compiled by The Blackdown Practice Patients' Participation Group with additions and updates by Local Parish Councils.

BISHOPSWOOD:

Bishopswood Chapel : Pastors Nyall & Beryl Davies 01460 234748
Short Mat Bowling - Weds even - Bishopswood Hall 01823 601262
Otterford and Bishopswood Womens Institute - lst. Thurs - Bishopswood Hall 01460 234560
Hand Bells - Betty Barker - 01823 601603 : Drama Group - Betty Barker - 01823 601603

BLACKBOROUGH and parts of KENTISBEARE

Parish Council-Mr.C. Warner 01884 34071 : St. Mary's Church Rev P. Sourbut 01884 33429
Bellringers - Mr J. Western 01884 266452 : Garden Club (Ch) Mr. J. Attfield 01884 266385
Blackborough Hall-Mr. B. Linfoot 01884 266453 : Brownies- Mrs L.Brown 01884 266643
Blackborough Womens Meeting - Mrs M. Edmond 01884 266415
Cricket Club- Mrs M Hinshelwood 01884 266500 : Football Club - D.Goff 01884 266597
Kentisbeare School - Mrs T Hailey (Head Teacher) 01884 266300
Village Hall - Mrs. J. Rookes 01884 266474 : Royal British Legion - J. Rowe 01884 266292
Womens Institute - Mrs A. Chappell 01884 266304 : Youth Club - D. Chave 01884 266222
Culm Valley Young Farmers - Mr. Blackmoor - 01884 266602
Sainthill Baptist Church - Rev M. Haighton 01884 266284

BLAGDON HILL & PITMINSTER:

Pitminster Church Bob Parker 421232 : Sarah Wakefield 01823 421461
Pitminster Cricket Club - Nick Williams Sat& Suns Sellicks Green 01823 283487
Sellicks Green Cricket Club - Eric Fogg Sats & Weds Sellicks Green 01823 421535
Fitness Exercising - Rosemary Hannam - Weds - Gatchell House,Trull 01823 421823
Women's Institute - 3rd Tuesday in month - Old School Pitminster 01823 421387
Play Group - Mrs. S. Spiller - Mon,Wed & Fri - Pitminster Primary School 01823 421720
Dancing - Robert Howe - Tues & Wed 7pm- Old School Pitminster 01823 421802
Corfe & Pitminster Historical Society - 3rd Tues 7.30pm- Old School 01823 421329

BUCKLAND ST. MARY:

Parish Council - G. Horner - 01460 234229 : Primary School-Mrs.J Baker -01460 234251
Pre School - Alison Rixon - 01460 234618 : Toddlers - Carole Cottey - 01460 234757
Newsletter - H. Cummings - 01460 234460 : Womens Institute - Val Lury - 01460 234394
Church of St. Mary's & Birchwood Chapel - Rev. Nan Shrimpton - 01823 601594
Reader -Mr Andrew Bell - 01460 324463 : Community Beat - D. Gorham - 01823 337911
Church Wardens - Mr. G. Board - 01460234200 : Mr. Ian Cumming - 01460 234460
Neighbourhood Watch - Mr. Bill Fairhurst - 01460 234456
Cricket Club- Jill Every - 01460 234604 : Venture Scouts- Mr. S. Layzel - 01460 54102
Brownies - Mrs. Del Wiggins - 01460234458 : Scouts - David Jefferies - 01823 601438
Guides - Elaine Jennings-01460 66364 : Royal British Legion - Mr. A.Bell-01460 234463
Yarty Gardening Club - Mary Pleeth - 01460 234560
Women's Institute - Mrs Valerie Lury - 3rd Tues - Village Hall 01460 234894
Toddlers - Mrs Karen Atkinson Pre school - Mrs Alison Rixon 01460 234618
Friends of Buckland School - Phil West : Chair of Govs - Mrs T. Croom 01460234718

CLAYHIDON:

St. Andrews Church - Rev. M. Cameron M.A. 01823 681189
Rosemary Lane Chapel - Mr. L Burston - 01823 680496
Clayhidon Council-T Blackmoor-01823 680485 : Village Hall-Mrs D. Pike 01823 680819
Neighbourhood Watch - J. Ward - 01823 680620:
Womens Institute-Miss J. Ward-01823 680620 : Toddlers-Mrs. M. Roberts 01823 680282
Bell Ringers - Mrs C Bendle - 01823 681047 : History - Mr. K. Wakeling 01823 680543

CHURCHSTANTON / CHURCHINFORD / STAPLEY:

Parish Council - Mr. B. Simpson - 2nd. Wed in month. Chunfrd Vill Hall 01823 601694
Churchstanton Parish Church - Rev Nan Shrimpton 01823 601594
CBO News - A. Dawson / D. Wright 01823 601422 - Adds - A. Winslade 01823 601344
Baptist Church - Mr. J.Woolam -Newhouse Chapel Smeatharpe 01404 861313
Blackdown Hills Riding Club - Kim Bale - 01823 601441
Womens' Institute - Gloria Dobinson lst Thurs - Smeatharpe Village Hall 01823 601256
Brownies & Guides - Del Wiggins - Fri's - Buckland St. Mary Village Hall 01460 234458
Cubs- Alison Vickery - Mons - Buckland St. Mary Village Hall 01823 334566
Scouts - Andy Champion - Mons - Buckland St. Mary Village Hall 01460 54166
Venture Scouts - Steve Layzell - Alt. Wednesdays - Buckland Village Hall 01460 54102
Aerobics - Alison Roberts - Churchinford Village Hall - Mon evens 01823 601567
Churchstanton Primary School - Mr. R. Bullock (Head Teacher) 01823 601354
Cricket Stuart Pitman-Churchinford C.C : 01823 278561 Nick Stilton-Colts -01823 601418
Gardening Club - Pam Kellett - Last Wednesday - Churchinford Vill Hall 01823 601530
Golden Age Mike Taylor lst & 3rd Wednesday - Churchinford Vill Hall 01823 601562
Keep Fit - Mary Humphries - Mon - Smeatharpe Village Hall 01823 680536
Pre-School - Sally Hodges - Mon/Wed/Fri Churchinford Village Hall 01823 234704
Royal British Legion - Mike Venn - 01823 601377
Bell Ringing - Gary Cooper 01823 286149 : History Group Geoffrey Berry - 01823 601451
Church Flower Arranging - Chris Hopcraft - 01823601451
HEALTH RELATED GROUPS - Contact Brian Simpson. BLKD Practice 01823 0681036

COMBE ST. NICHOLAS

Parish Council - Mrs A. Hunt - 01460 61449 : Parish Church - Rev. Regan 01460 62121
Methodist Church - Mr. B. Hodge - 01460 65149 : Village Hall - Mr. Bailey 01460 65376
Parish News - Mrs. B. Cloke - 01460 01460 : Gala Assoc - Mrs. Miller 01460 65855
Senior Citizens Club - Mrs. Dethridge - 01460 64452
Playgroup - Mrs. Barrett 01460 67803 : Local Ladies - Mrs. S. Boyle 01460 6162

COMBE ST. NICHOLAS **continued**

Cricket - Mr. P. Harris - 01460 63915 : Football - Mr. I. Hutchings 01460 234396
Short Mat Bowls - Gill Coleman - 01460 63188 : Xmas Tree - Mrs A Miller 01460 65855
Horticultural Society - Mrs Trayford - 01460 62251 : Flower Show (Aug) 01460 67407

CULMSTOCK
Football - Steven Thresher 01884 840100 : Cricket Patrick Eariand 01884840438
Keep Fit - Lovis Alford - Thurs - Village Hall - 01884840557
Baptist Church - Kenneth Cox - 01884 840728 - Methodist - George Hitch 01884 840534
Church of England - Rev Magaret Cameron M.A.- 01884 840358
Brownies - Jane Hayes-Pamshaw - Mon - evenings - Village Hall 01884 842121
Wives Club -Pam Shaw - lst Wed in month - 01884841121 - Hazel Barrow 01884 840698
Women's Institute - Janet Connolly -3rd Tuesday in month - Village Hall 01884 840366
Evergreens - Jean O'Connor - 2nd Thursday in month - Village Hall 01884 840808
Playgroup - Pam Shaw - Mon,Tues,Wed,Thurs - Methodist School 01884 841121
HEALTH RELATED GROUPS - Contact Person - Millicent Perkins 01884 840358

DALWOOD
St. Peters Parish Church : Dalwood Methodist Chapel
Dalwood Fayre - Street Fair 3 rd Sat in August, held under ancient Charter.

DUNKESWELL
Parish Council - Clerk - Charles Sumpter - Village Hall - 01404 891284
Pre - School Mrs. Veronica Layzell 01404 42183
Dunkeswell & Sheldon Parish News - Richard Broad - 01404 891608
Village Hall Committee - Mrs Cynthia Broad - (Sec) - Varies - 01404 891608
Womens' Institute - Pres. Heather Sweetland - Vill Hall - 01823 680287
Church of England Vicar - Rev Nick Wall - 01404 891243
Chapel - Edwin Froggatt - 01404 891237 - Sunday School - Carol Quinain 01404 891291
Neighbourhood Watch - Main co-ordinator - Richard Broad 01404 891608
Highfield Sports & Social Club - Sec - Mrs Kath Strickland - 01404 891439
Dunkeswell Rovers Football Team - Sec - Mrs Marion Broom - 01404891377
Dunkeswell Youth Football Club - Paul Mansfield 01404 890084
Badminton - Mr Nichols - 01404891950 Tennis - Mrs. Di Peak- 01404 891522
Bowling Club - Derek Viles - 01404 891484
Bell ringers - Charles Sumpter - 01404 891284 : Keep Fit - S. Freemantle - 01404 891428
Beavers - Mrs L Barnes 5-8 years - Mon - Community Hall - 01404 891572
Cubs and Scouts - Mrs McMullan - Mons - Community Hall 8-11 years - 01404 891370
Gardening Association - Tony Lubbock - Last Tues/month- Vill Hall - 01404 891797
Community Hall Bookings - Eddie Harding - 01404 891816
Sheldon Singers - Julie D'Ath-Lancaster - Thurs evens - Sheldon Vill Hall - 01404 841583
Village Hall Events - Wassail, Bonfire Nights, Concerts, Lamb Roast etc - 01404 891608
Flower Show - Spring & Summer Garden Soc - 01404 891797.

HEMYOCK
Parish Council- Mr. B. Clyst - 01823 680289
Parish Church St. Mary's - Rev M.Cameron - 01823 680244
Baptist Church - Pastor Michael Jarrett - 01823 680946
Parish Hall - Mrs. Y. Pike - 01823 680068 : St. Mary's Ringers - Mrs L. Holway - 680708
Rosemary Lane Chappel & Bolhan Chapel - Mr. L. Burston 01823 680496
Neighbourhood Watch - Mr. D. Goddard - 01823 680107
County Councilor- Mrs C. Bulley 01823 681075 : Over 60's - Mrs J. Austin - 01823 680882
District Councillor - Mrs. H. Stallard - 01823 680237
Primary School - Mrs G. Peters (Head teacher) - 01823 680240
Badminton Club - Mrs .Phillips- 0182368065 : Bowls - Mr. D. McCulloch- 01823 680365
Cricket - Mr T Slator - 01823 680932 : Football - Mr T. Humphries - 01823 680536
Keep Fit- Mrs. M. Humphries- 01823 680536 : Snooker - Mr L Bowden- 01823 680106
Tennis - Mrs S Lambert - 01823 680664 : Ringers - Mrs L Holway - 01823 680708
Cubs - Mrs S Phillips - 01823 680652 : Guides - Mrs. K. Williams - 01884 841354
Scouts - Mr J. Northam - 01884 672 789 : Venture Scouts - Mr. Shepherd - 01823 680744
St Mary's Guild - Mrs J. Llewellyn -Jones - 01823 680592
Carnival Commitee - Mrs K. Pinder - 01823 681034
Women's Institute - Mrs. E. Hotten - 01823 680479
Young Farmers - Diane Ward - 01823 672081 : Cameo Club- Mrs A Monk - 01823 680882
Mums & Toddlers - Mrs L. Pullman - 01823 680065
Hemyock Playschool and Playgroup - Mrs J. Doble - 01823 680174
Hemyock Singers - Mrs J Bawler - Tues evening - Forbes Lounge -01823 680352
Blackdown Support Group - Mr Brian Simpson - The Surgery - 01823 681036

MEMBURY:
Primary School - Head Teacher - Mrs Weatherley - 01404 881491.
Churchwardens - Mrs M. Burrough - 01404 881393 or Mrs.Tapp - 01404 881368
Parish Hall - Mr. C. Abbott - 01404 881638 : British Legion - Mr. R. Rath -01404 861329
Footpath Warden - Mr. A.Scott- Nash 01404 881645
Local History Society - Mrs. M. Phillimore -01404 881430
Arts and Crafts - Mrs. R. Abrahams - 01404 881677
Short Mat Bowls - Mrs J. Johnson - 01297 35786

MONKTON
Womens Institute - Mrs M Bright - 01404 41807

LUPPITT
St. Mary's Church & Village Hall - Mrs Pearl Pulman - 01404 891324

VILLAGE COMMUNITY INFORMATION

SHELDON
Parish Meeting - Mr. R. Cook -01404 841592 : Village Hall Mr. G. Hicks - 01404 841356
Youth Club - Mr Wilf Stoyie - Vill Hall Wed pm : Neighbourhood Watch - 01404 841356
Sheldon Singers Mrs J. D'ath-Lancaster - Thurs evenings - Village Hall - 01404 891583

SMEATHARPE
Parish Council - John Cornish
Whist- Neil Kellett - Fortnightly -Tues Village Hall - 01823 601530
Womens' Institute - Mrs. G.Small - 1st Thurs - Village Hall - 01823 601216
Keep Fit - Mrs. M.Humphries - Mons - 01823 680536
Newhouse Baptist Church - Mr. J.Wooliam Sundays & Tues eve - 0404 801313

STOCKLAND
St Michael and All Angels- Priest in Charge 01297-33156
Stockland Fair & Donkey Derby - 01404 881447 : Royal British Legion - 01404 881698
Stockland & district Horticultural Society - 01404 861394 : Tennis Club - 01404 861394
Stockland Womens Institute 01404 831673 : Cricket Club - 01404 43342

UFFCULME
Parish Council-Mr. F. Welland-01884 840152 : Parish Church-Rev. J. Bird 01884 841001
Womens Institute-Mrs.Scantlebury 01884 841731 : Firework display - 01884 840282
Church Fete- the Vicar 01884 841001 : Summer Show-P.Spearing-01884 35021
Bowling Club- B. Gatford- 01823 840614 :

UPOTTERY
Parish Council
Football - Daniel Prettyjohn - 01404 891477 : Cricket - Philip Joyce - 01404 891328
Indoor Bowls - Neil Kellet- 01823 601530 :Tennis - J.Chilcott & W. Drew- 01823 601368
Womens' Institute - Gill Thomas 2nd Thurs - Manor Room - 01404 861406
PCC Sec: - FA Wigram - 01404 891229 : Play Group - Gillian Broom - 01404 831253
Art - Gwengar Smart - 01404 861309 : Craft - Vivian Weston - 01404 861453

WAMBROOK
Wambrook Flower & Family Dog Show : Sat July : E. Jackson - 014606 3350

YARCOMBE
Parish Council- Mrs. M.Smith- 01404 861541:Womens Inst- Mrs. D.Baker-01404 861557
St.John's Church Rev.J.Stone 01404 861561 : Baptist Chapel Mrs.Warren- 01404 861401
Skittles - Mrs. L.Sutton - 01404 861386 : Cricket - Mr. I. Rich - 01404 861274
Mothers' Union- Mrs. W.Rattenbury- 01404 861443 :
Whist Drives-Mrs.J.Symes-01404 8613644 -Melody Makers-Mrs. M.Lane-01404 861401
Royal British Legion - Mr. R. Routh - 01404 861329

YAK Yarcombe Amenities Club- Mrs. L.Lutton Senior Citizens - 01404 861386
Sunday School-Mrs. Lutton-01404 861386 : Young Farmers Club. Mr. Key-01404 861278
SKY Singing Kids of Yarcombe - Mrs. L. Freeman - 01404 861541

WEST BUCKLAND
Parish Council-Mr. E. Harding 01823 667291 : Primary School-Mr. Grace-01823 663376
Parish Church - Rev. D. Randell 01823 664925 : Village Hall - P.Sellick - 01823 665763
Womens Institute- Mrs H. Shove 01823 663990 : Village Fete- Mr. N.Stag- 01823 664545

ACCOMMODATION : BED & BREAKFAST

Awliscombe - Mrs.T. Layzell, Lelamarie - 01404 44646.
Awliscombe - Mrs. Manley, Birds Frm - 01404 841262.

Mrs. Molly I. Bennett - (Sponsor Page 61)
Lane End Farm.
Broadhembury - 01404 841563.

William & Anne Barons - (Sponsors Page 13)
STAFFORD BARTON - BROADHEMBURY
Quality en-suite Farmhouse Bed & Breakfast
Table license : 3 Crowns H.C. - **01404 841403**

Sarah & Roger at - ***(Sponsors Page 14)***
HAWTHORNE HOUSE - *BISHOPSWOOD*
Bed and Breakfast - Open all year round - **01460 234482**

KEYMER COTTAGE - Buckland St. Mary
Victorian Farmhouse Bed & Breakfast
(Sponsors Page 31) H.C. Hospitality Services - 01460 234460

Combe Raleigh - Mrs. D. Retter, The Pheasantry - 01404 42130.
Combe Raleigh /Luppitt - Mrs. M.Turrell, Pulshays - 01404 891326.
Combe Raleigh - Mrs.M.Rickson, Sunnyside Farm - 01404 43489.

Miss. W. Ambrose. - The York Inn **- Churchinford**
En-suite accommodation with fine traditional hospitality
01823 601333. 16th. century Inn **(Sponsor Page 29)**

Churchstanton - **Pear Tree Cottage** ***- Stapley.***
Thatched Country Cottage - (Sponsor Page 5)
Pam Parry Welcomes You All Year Round
Tel & Fax - 01823 601224 : E-mail colvin.parry@virgin.net

Highfield - HAZELDEAN - Dunkeswell
Mrs. Eileen Marks - 01404 891648

Cotleigh - Mrs. P. Boyland, Barn Park Farm -01404 861297.
Luppitt - Mrs. A.Krestoynikoff, Jacks House - 01404 891341.
Hemyock - Mrs. A.Sworn, Orchard Lea - 01823 680057.

THE SQUARE- *Brook House* -HEMYOCK
(Sponsor Page 56) - *Bed & Breakfast in the Village Square*
For Reservations telephone - **01823 680811.**

Pitminster - Mr & Mrs. M. Jerrold, Coach House - 01823 421571.
Upottery - Mrs. J. Tucker, Yard Farm - 01404 861680.
Upottery - Mrs. E. Tucker, Lower Luxton Frm - 01823 601269.

Upottery - COURTMOOR FARM - (Sponsor Page 25)
Quality Bed & Breakfast Accommodation - Spectacular Views
En-suite shower rooms - Colour Tv - Coffee & tea making facilities
Bob & Rosalind Buxton - Tel: 01404 861565 Fax: 01404 861564

Upottery - *ROBINS COTTAGE* - (Sponsor Page 28)
En-suite Thatched Cottage Accommodation in a
Delightful Devon Village Setting
Theresa Foster : Telephone 01404 861281

Smeatharpe - Lower Southey Farm - (Sponsor Page 64)
Mrs. Joyce Lockyer - *Home from home accommodation*
Children welcome - Evening Meal by arrangement
On the Culmhead to Dunkeswell road : Tel: 01823 601331

Wambrook - Mrs. J.K.Eames, Wambrook Farm- 01460 62371.

WAMBROOK -WOODVIEW- (Sponsor Page 83)
Bed & Breakfast in a Victorian School House in an idyllic village setting
Mrs. Jenny Reynolds - **Tel 01460 65368**

Wambrook - Mrs Johnson - Weston Farm - 01460 63358.
Wilmington - Mrs C. Hudson,The Old Forge - 01404 831297.

Yarcombe - Crawley Frm - Mrs. 1. Dyer
On the A30 between Chard and Honiton - 01404 64760.

ACCOMMODATION : HOTELS

The Belfry Hotel, Yarcombe, Honiton - 01404 861234.

The Lea Hill Hotel
MEMBURY
' Winner of the Sunday Times Golden Pillow Award
Traditional English Food with a Pacific Rim Influence
Open to non residents : Booking essential
(Sponsor Page 78) Tel: **01404 881881**

The Olde English Pub Co. presents
The George Hotel & Conference Centre,
(Tytherleigh Cot Hotel) **Chardstock Nr. Axminster, Devon.**
(Sponsors Page 84) Hotel - 01460 221170. Inn - 01460 220241

ACCOMMODATION : SELF CATERING

TIMBERTOP & HOEMOOR
Self Catering Bungalows
On real working farms
CHURCHINFORD
Mrs. Manning Mrs. Phillips
Open all year round
01823 601378/601265.
(Sponsors Page 70)

Hemyock -Mrs. A. Edwards, Chapel Frm Cottage - 01823 680430.
Hemyock - Mrs Stephney, Bakers Cottage - 01823 680408.
Hemyock - Mrs. C. King, Dunns Green Farm - 01823 680447.
Membury - Mrs. P. Steel, Haslands Frm - 01404 881558.
Otterford - Mr. P Wright .Rull Farm - 01460 234398
WAMBROOK - PULLEYS BARN, HIGHER WAMBROOK - 01460 65283.
West Buckland - Mrs. K. Male, Londsdale - 01823 421386.

Sheldon - *Hollies Trout Farm* - Mrs. J. M. Roles
Log Cabin in idyllic settings (Sponsor Cover) Tel : 01404 841428.

Smeatharpe - PIPISTRELLE HOUSE - Rob & Angela Lockyer
Traditional Barn Cottages at the heart of the Blackdowns
On the Culmhead to Dunkeswell road Tel: 01823 601554.

ACCOMMODATION : CARAVANS & CAMPING

Andrewshayes Caravan Park Off the A35 : Taunton Cross, Dalwood, Devon. - 01404 831225.

FOREST GLADE
(Sponsor Back Cover)
Cullompton Devonshire
Tel: 01404 841381
Fax: 01404 841593
International Caravan & Camping Park

FISHPONDS HOUSE (Sponsors Page 60)
DUNKESWELL
Rick and Tracy
Camping : Fishing : Pub
Restaurant : Functions
Tel: 01404 891358

Holly Bush Caravan Park, Culmhead - 01823 421515.

South Somerset Holiday Park
3 miles west of Chard : The old A30 Turnpike
Bob & Doreen Weeks : Camping & Touring
(Sponsors Page 74) : Telephone 01460 66036/62221

ATTRACTIONS : PUBS & RESTAURANTS

Air Centre - Dunkeswell Airfield. - 01404 891226

THE *Brook House* TAKE AWAY- HEMYOCK
OPENING TIMES - Wed, Thur, Fri, Sat - 12 am - 2pm and 6 pm - 9.30 pm
FISH'N CHIPS - CURRY - PIZZA & LOTS - LOTS MORE
(Sponsor Page 56) - FOR ORDERS TEL: **01823 680811.**

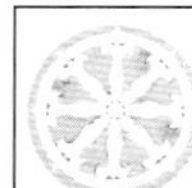

THE CATHERINE WHEEL
Hemyock - Geoff Taylor - (Sponsor P 57)
- Fine hospitality and food -
For Reservations - 01823 680224

Candlelight Inn, Bishopswood. - 01823 234476
Cotley Arms, Wambrook. - 01460 62348.

CULM VALLEY INN
Culmstock : Lance Prince : (Sponsor P 55)
GOOD FOOD IN A CHARACTER ATMOSPHERE
01884 840354

Drewe Arms
(SPONSOR PAGE 62)
BROADHEMBURY
01404 841267
Drewe Arms

ATTRACTIONS : PUBS & RESTAURANTS

(SponsorsPage 88) 'THE BUNKER CAFE' Marcus Rd.
The Airfield Dunkeswell : Open 7 days a week from 8 am.
Outside Catering Available. : Telephone : - 01404 890025

Eagle Tarvern, Buckland St Mary. - 01823 234292.
Flintlock, Marsh. - 01823 234403.

FISHPONDS HOUSE
DUNKESWELL Rick and Tracy
Camping : Fishing : Pub : Restaurant : Functions
(Sponsor Page 60) - **Tel: 01404 891358**

Green Dragon, Coombe St Nicholas. - 01460 63311.

The Olde English Pub Co. presents
The George Inn at Chardstock
Quality food and ale in a traditional Thatched Pub & Restaurant
(Sponsors Page 84) Hotel - 01460 221170. Inn - 01460 220241

THE HIGHFIELD FISH PLAICE RESTAURANT
(Sponsor Page 58) - DUNKESWELL - TAKE AWAY
Mon - Sat Lunch 10am- 1.45 pm. Mon - Sat - Eve 5.30pm - 9.30pm.
Sunday Roast - 12 am - 2 pm - Tel : **01404 891866**

Staple - The Greyhound Inn - Fitzpaine.
Real Ales and Introducing our Speciality Dishes in the Restaurant : En- suite Bed & Breakfast.
(Sponsor Page 51) - Tel: 01823 480227.

Culmhead - Holman Clavel - Staple Hill.
RICHARD, CARA, RICHARD AND CHIMNEY CHARLIE INVITE YOU TO DINE ON FINE FRESH FISH AND DRINK GREAT ALE IN THE FAMOUS BLACKDOWN PUB.
(Sponsor Page 47) - Tel: 01823 421432.

THE HOWLEY TAVERN *at* Howley

Bed & Breakfast : A la Carte Restaurant
(Sponsors P 23) - ***Real Ales - Snacks***
Ken & Diana Leaf - Tel: **01460 62157**

The Ilminster Stage
17th century Coaching Inn-Culmstock
En-suite B&B - Restaurant - Real Ales
TEL: 01884 840872. Peter &Jenny - (Sponsors P 54)

The Kings Arms Inn
AT STOCKLAND
En-suite Bed & Breakfast - Restaurant & Traditional Bars
(Sponsors Page 81) : Tel - 01404 881361. Fax 01404 881732

Half Moon, Clayhidon. - 01823 680291.
Haymaker, Coombe St. Nicholas - 01460 64161.

Luppit Inn, Luppit.
Monkton Court, Monkton. - 01404 42309.
Merry Harriers, Forches Corner. - 01823 421270.
The Ostler, Uffculme. - 01884 840260

THE LAMB AND FLAG

Circa 1647 - Blagdon Hill.
(Sponsors 33) : David & Val Lacey
Fine Food : Beer Garden : Skittles - TEL: 01823 421736

Furely -The Longbridge Inn- Membury
Teresa & Alan welcome you to Real Ales, Fine Wines, an extensive Bar & Restaurant Menu, Skittles, Pool and Games. Walkers welcome
(Sponsors Page 82) - Tel: 01404 81366.

THE SIDMOUTH ARMS
Pete & Liz Rigler AT UPOTTERY (Sponsors P 71)
BED & BREAKFAST : RESTAURANT
FUNCTION ROOM TEL: 01404 861252.

The Queens Arms at PITMINSTER.
TRADITIONAL BAR AND FINE FOOD IN THE RESTAURANT
Simon & Emma Callow - (Sponsors P 36) - 01823 421529

Dunkeswell THE ROYAL OAK Dunkeswell
SUNDAY CARVERY : RESTAURANT
Traditional Food and Ale in a Homely Atmosphere
Maria Howard (Sponsor Page 59) **Tel: 01404 891280.**

The Tuckers Arms at Dalwood
Thatched Bed & Breakfast Accommodation
Fine English Food and Ales - Fax 01404 881802
David & Kate Beck **(Sponsors P79) -Tel: 01404 881342**

The White Lion Blagdon Hill
Good food in a traditional Pub
Brian & Becky Hinton
(Sponsors P 38) Tel: 01823 421296.

Malcolm & Jeanne Weech welcome you to White Hart Inn at Corfe.
Home made Food, Skittles Alley, Conferences, Weddings, Fine Ales
(Sponsors p48) **Tel: 01823 421388.**

THE YARCOMBE INN
Yarcombe, Devon : Katherine & Simon
Pub Chef of the Year 1995
(Sponsors P21) **Bookings recommended 01404 861676**

The York Inn at **Churchinford.**
Fine Food and Real ales
En-suite Bed and Breakfast Accommodation
Wendy & Reg -Sponsors P 29-**Tel: 01823 601333**

ATTRACTIONS/LEISURE GENERAL

Allhallows Museum High St. Honiton - 01404 44966
Chard ' Stringfellow & Agricultural' Museum 01460 67463
Coldhabour Mill Uffculme, Working Wool Museum - 01884 840960
Dunkeswell Memorial Museum, Dunkeswell Airfield - 01404 891943

THE WELCOME CENTRE
CHRIS & JANE INVITE YOU TO ENJOY
- **RIDING AT HEAZLE STABLES**
- **VISITOR INFORMATION & CAFE**
- **EVENTS IN HEAZLE ARENA**

(Sponsor P 41) TELEPHONE 01823 680280

Hemyock Castle, Hemyock. By appointment - 01823 680745.
Ferne Animal Sanctuary,Tea Shop, Wambrook - 01460 65214.
Wellington Museum - 01823 664747.

ATTRACTIONS/LEISURE FLYING

Adventure Ballooning, Buckland St. Mary - 01460 234597.
Devon & Somerset Balloons - 01823 698757.

PILOT A LIGHT AIRCRAFT
AIR EXPERIENCE FLIGHTS FROM £32
GIFT VOUCHERS AVAILABLE FOR FREE BROCHURE
THE DEVON SCHOOL OF FLYING (Sponsor Page 18)
THE IDEAL PRESENT
Choose from a 2 or 4 seat modern Aircraft
TEL 01404 891643
Dunkeswell Aerodrome . Nr. Honiton

Somerset Microlights - Dunkeswell - 01823 442391.
Dawn Patrol, Vintage Biplanes, Aerobatics - 0836 650357.
Devon and Somerset Gliding Club - Sheldon - 01404 841386.
Devon & Somerset Parachute School - 01404 891690.

ATTRACTIONS FISHING

Harts BeerLake Trout Fishery, Culm Davy - Hemyock - 01823 680319.

HOLLIES TROUT FARM & FISHERY
FLY & COARSE FISHING LAKES
FRESH TROUT : SMOKED TROUT
SMOKED TROUT PATE
SELF CATERING LOG CABIN TO RENT
SHELDON (Sponsor Front Cover) **Tel: 01404 841428.**

FISHPONDS HOUSE DUNKESWELL
Rick and Tracy **RESTAURANT** (Sponsors P. 60)
FISHING : CAMPING : ACCOMMODATION
FUNCTIONS : BARS : TEL: 01404 891358.

ATTRACTIONS/LEISURE GOLF

Taunton & Pickeridge Golf Club, Corfe - 01823 421537.
Axecliff Golf Club, Axmouth - 01297 20499.
Honiton Golf Club, Middle Hills - 01404 42943.

ATTRACTIONS — GOLF

OTTER VALLEY GOLF CENTRE
- At Rawridge -
INDOOR FACILITY : 9 PRACTICE HOLES
P.G.A. APPROVED TEACHING CENTRE
Golf Pro-Andrew Thompson PGA.
(Sponsor P 72) - Tel: 01404 861266

ACCOUNTANTS

Lentells-Mr. A.Stallard ACA-Hemyock - 01823 286274/681192

AGRICULTURAL CONTRACTORS

C.J.Barrow
ALSO SKID STEER HIRE
(Sponsor P26) - DUNKESWELL 01404 891510 / 0468 025274

DAVID LOCK (Sponsor P 67)
BIG Sqr & Rnd Baling & Wrapping, Ploughing,
Pwr Harrowing, Hedge Trimming & LGP Fertilising
Telephone - 0467447121

Yarcombe - George Pigeon 01404 881634

AGRICULTURAL ENGINEERS

Denleys Agricultural Engineers, Awliscombe- 01404 841311

GD ENGINEERING-HEMYOCK-GARETH DEAR
AGRICULTURAL ENGINEERING & FABRICATION
(Sponsor Page 24)
Tel: 07971 408832

G.H. & E.J HAWKINS (Sponsor P 86)
AGRICULTURAL & CAR REPAIRS
Silver St. Cumstock. Devon 01884840781

Roy Sampson - All Makes Serviced - 01404 861621
Yarcombe - Hilltop Services - 01404 861525 / 0802 370385
Yarcombe - Richard Briant - 01404 861371

AGRICULTURAL FARM SUPPLIES

BLACKDOWN FARM SUPPLIES NICK AND RUTH STRANGE BEECH HAYES FRM.
FEEDS : FRESH MEAT & POULTRY
(Sponsor p2) - CHURCHINFORD - Tel - 01823 601565

Procter's Woodflakes : Dunkeswell - 01404 891245

ANTIQUES

Pughs Farm Antiques, Pughs Farm, Monkton - 01404 42860

COLYSTOCK • ANTIQUES •
STOCKLAND
A visit to our showroom is highly recommended
Sponsors Page 80
Tel/Fax 01404 861271

BOARDING KENNELS & CATTERIES

Ashculme Boarding Kennels - Hemyock. - 01823 6804272

FOXDOWN DOG TRAINING CENTRE - Culmhead
Dog Training, Boarding, Rescue. Tel : 01823 601532

Hartshill Kennels and Cattery-Bewley Down - 01460 220343

Yarcombe - **KATKINS** - Boarding Cattery
WOODSIDE, YARCOMBE Tel: 01404 861503

BUILDING CONTRACTORS

Awliscombe: J.R. Layzell & Sons - 01404 42308/ 44646
Broadhembury - B.G. Middleton - 01404 841495
Blackdowns Roofing Co.Ltd-01823 289951 / 01404 891525
Churchinford : D.W. Winslade Builder - 01823 601136
Churchstanton : Willand Elm - 01823 601212/ 0378 743698
Dunkeswell :T&T Building Services- 01404 891098/891136
Dunkeswell-Meads Building - 01404 890058 / 0441 192285
Hemyock : Thomas Morgan - 01823 6805983

Denis W.Hart & Son
A TRADITION OF FINE BUILDING
ON THE BLACKDOWNS
(Sponsor P40) - Tel: 01823 680120

REDWOOD & SONS CLAYHIDON
HEATING INSTALLATIONS & SERVICING
PURPOSE MADE JOINERY : FUNERAL DIRECTORS
FMB (Sponsors P42) Tel : 01823 680268 / 680571

ROOKS CASTLE CONSTRUCTION
PLUMBING:FLOORING
: EXTENSIONS :
: STONEWORK :
FARM BUILDINGS
34 YRS EXPERIENCE
ROOFING : JOINERY
CARPENTRY:ELECTRIC'S
SPONSOR P 45
01823 601408
01823 667758

Yarcombe - Chris Doble - 01404 861324
Yarcombe - W.E. Phillips & Sons - 01404 861364
Yarcombe - David Pitwood - 01404 881700

BUILDING SUPPLIES

FRM BUILDING SUPPLIES
JOHN CARR : (Sponsor P 63)
THE AIRPORT
Dunkeswell
Tel : 01404 891247
FRM BUILDING SUPPLIES

CARPENTRY & JOINERY

Chardstock- Bob Dunn - Chardstock Works - 01460 221148
John Bimson - Garden Barrows-See page 9 - 01823 680395

CHURCHILLS
Patio Canopies · Conservatories · Fitted Kitchens · Windows & Doors
PURPOSE MADE JOINERY
HEMYOCK (SPONSOR PAGE 32)
01823 680385 / 0421 354706

PRING & SON of HEMYOCK
FURNITURE SPECIALIST & JOINERY
MADE TO YOUR DESIGN : (SPONSORS P 16)
Tel : 01823 680405 : Mobile 0860 390002

Hemyock : D.J. Bawler - No Job too Small 01823 680352

Richard Foster - WOODWORKER
UPOTTERY
Tel : 01404 861 281
(Sponsor P 66)

ROB LOCKYER PIPISTRELLE HOUSE, SMEATHARPE
Hand crafted Windows : Doors : Staircases : Paneling.
JOINERY TO ORDER - Tel. 01823 601554

Mark Staple-Quality Joinery - 01460 234200/ 01823 322245

CAR SALES

LUXTON 4X4
CHARLIE HOPCRAFT
Be Outwardbound not Snowbound
(Sponsor P8) 01823 601584

DOBLES GARAGE : David E. Graham
HEMYOCK : (SPONSOR P 4) Tel : 01823 680233

IMTEC- Performance Cars - Dunkeswell - 01404 891900

P. SPARKS GARAGE BLAGDON HILL (Sponsor p37)
SUZUKI SPECIALISTS - Tel : 01823 421606

CAR & MOTOR REPAIRS

G. H. & E. J. HAWKINS
AGRICULTURAL & CAR REPAIRS
SILVER STREET . CULMSTOCK. DEVON
(Sponsor P 86) - Tel: 01884 840781

CAR & MOTOR REPAIRS

Dunkeswell E & A Motors, Marcus Rd. - 01404 891920
Kentisbeare - Auto Culm Services - 01884 266641
Luppit - Geoff Clyst - Vehicle Technician - 01404 891256
Yarcombe Coachworks - 01460 61927

CATERERS

Sugar Spice Creative Cooking — A Personal Service — Weddings Parties
Sponsor Page 52 Tel 01823 662292

THE PROPER PUDDING COMPANY
Fresh Homemade Sweets & Puddings made on the Blackdown Hills.
Sponsor Page 20 - Tel: 01823 421468

CHIMNEY SWEEPS

Peter Ferrari, Churchinford - 01823 601419

CLEANING SERVICES

Town & country Cleaning Services - 01404 861512

CLERICAL SERVICES -

FIRST CHOICE - Office Services - 01404 891154
Flights of Fancy Interior Decorations- 01823 601451

COMMERCIAL VEHICLES

Marsh Motors - Sales Repairs - 01460 234216
Gerald Lye - Heavy Vehicle Repairs - 01404 861260

COMPUTERS AND I.T.

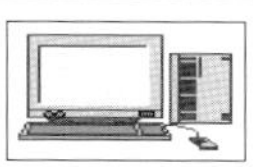

P.C. broken -Or Just Slow?
BARRY COLLINS
01404 841672
No Call out Charge! On-site Service, No Fix - No Fee !

CURTAINING

Curtains with Care -Angela Perry - 01823 680373

DISTRIBUTION

RICHARD WEAVER Independent Distributor
for Healthcare Products, Leisure & Educational Books
CDs : Puzzles : (Sponsor p50) *Lifestyles Products* - intra
Tel: 01823 601 420 ECOFLOW

DOG TRAINING

FOXDOWN DOG TRAINING CENTRE - 01823 601532
Dog Training, : Boarding : Rescue. CULMHEAD

DRIVING SCHOOLS

AJL Heavy Goods Vehicle Tuition - 01823 601569
NoL's Ltd Phil Goodall - Dunkeswell - 01404 890017
VCP School of Motoring - 01884 841565

ESTATE AGENCIES

WILKIE & MOORES " Your Local Team Estate Agent"
Hemyock - 01823 680000 : Cullompton - 01884 35588

EDUCATION & TRAINING

Litework - Media Training
Personalised Computer training on Word, Clarisworks, PhotoShop & Quark Express. Video production training with Beta Sp, Hi 8 & Media 100.
Mike Drury Beck Cert Ed / D32/33 - (Sponsor p44) - **Tel: 01823 601679**

ELECTRICAL CONTRACTORS

Barley Meade Electrical Services
Tony Drawert - Sponsor Page 65
Domestic : Industrial : Farm Installations
Heating : Testing & Inspections
01823 680137 / 0411 116218

C. Cox Electrical Contractors - 01884 840728/01823 680276
Ray Gubb - Sales and Repairs - 01884 266295

FARM SHOPS

HIGHLANDS FARM SHOP
DOROTHY & IVOR - SMEATHARPE - Sponsors p68
Fresh Fruit & Veg, Cream, Preserves, Plants & Composts - Eggs & Ice Cream
TELEPHONE : **01823 601296**

HILL FARM SHOP
HOME OF MONUMENT VENISON
Opposite Quarts Moor : Clayhidon
FOR A COMPLETE RANGE OF NATURAL MEATS
(Sponsor Page 39) Tel : **01823 680307**

BEECH HAYES FARM: NICK AND RUTH STRANGE
FRESH MEAT & POULTRY : FARM FEEDS
(Sponsor p2) - **CHURCHINFORD - Tel - 01823 601565**

NORTHDOWN HOUSE FRM - Turkeys - 01823 601400
Sheldon Valley Farm Turkeys - 01404 841672

FETES AND FAIRS

Doodle Bug - Stalls for Fetes
Percentage of Sales Given to host organisations.
Jewellery : Party Bags & Fund raiser Discounts.
Sponsor Page 76 : 01404 881549

FLORISTS

'SAY IT WITH FLOWERS'
YOUR FLORIST FOR WEDDINGS
FUNERALS AND GIFTS
Dunkeswell - Tel:01404 890013

FISHMONGERS & FISHERIES

FISH DELIVERIES FOR THE BLACKDOWNS
FROSTS Fishmongers
BUCKLAND ST. MARY & READING
(Sponsors P 30) **01460 234621 / 234613**

Goodiford Mill Trout Farm & Fishery - 01884 266233
King Neptunes Catch : - 01460 234776 / 0802 708423

HOLLIES TROUT FARM & FISHERY
FLY & COARSE FISHING LAKES
FRESH TROUT : SMOKED TROUT
SMOKED TROUT PATE
SELF CATERING LOG CABIN TO RENT
SHELDON (Sponsor Front Cover) **Tel: 01404 841428.**

Membury Rock Mill Trout Farm . - 01404 881472 / 437

FINANCIAL SERVICES & INVESTMENTS

BLACKDOWN FINANCIAL SERVICES
Steve & Doreen Moores (Sponsors P6)
INDEPENDENT FINANCIAL ADVISERS
Investments : Pensions : Life Assurance
HALIFAX HOUSE : HEMYOCK
Telephone - 01823 680846
A member of Countrywide Independent Advisers Ltd. which is regulated by the Personal Investment Authority for life assurance, pensions & investment business only

Peter Samways (Sponsor Page 34)
STAFFORD HOUSE INVESTMENTS LTD
INDEPENDENT LIFE, PENSIONS & INVESTMENT SPECIALISTS
01832 256811 - 0831 773109
Regulated by the Personal Investment Authority

FORESTRY

CVT Forestry Services - 01884 841927
Durston Forestry - 01823 412131

FORESTRY

RICHARD BALL
FORESTRY CONTRACTOR
TREE & HEDGE MAINTENANCE
(Sponsor Page 49) - Tel: 01823 664553

FUNERAL SERVICES

J.R. Layzell & Sons, Awliscombe - 01404 42308 / 44646

Culm Valley Funeral Services Ltd. Hemyock. (Sps 16)
LINDA A. ISSAC : MARTIN PRING 01823 680405 / 0860 390002

Redwoods Funeral Director : Clayhidon. (Sps 42)
L.G. Redwood : A.F. Redwood 01823 680268 / 01823 680571

FURNITURE REST. & CABINET MAKERS

Alan Peters, Kentisbeare - 01884 266251

A.P.D. CROWE - (Sponsor Page 43)
CABINET MAKER
& FURNITURE RESTORER.
BLAGDON HILL : Tel : 01823 421443

PRING & SON of HEMYOCK
FURNITURE SPECIALIST & JOINERY
MADE TO YOUR DESIGN : (SPONSORS P 16)
Tel : 01823 680405 : Mobile 0860 390002

Tom Kealy, Buckland St. Mary. - 01460 234473.

GATES AND RAILINGS

ANDREW CLEGG - Metalworks to Order
WROUGHT IRON GATES & RAILINGS
Gate Automation - Tel/Fax 01460 62583

GARAGES & FILLING STATIONS

COMBE GARAGE : Underway, Combe St. Nicholas.
Garage, MOT's, Repairs.
UNIPART CAR CARE CENTRE : Tel: 01460 62126

CULMSTOCK GARAGE, CULMSTOCK.
(Sponsors Page 7) D.W. Rice & P. D. Rice
Recovery, Repairs, Servicing , Mot's &
Fine Engine Tuning - 01884 840570/ 840754

HIGHFIELD GARAGE DUNKESWELL
Servicing, Fuel, Shop. : Tel: 01404 891258

DOBLES GARAGE. Hemyock, Devon.
CAR SALES : MOT's : Service & Repairs.
' PEUGEOT SPECIALISTS'
(Sponsor page 4) **Tel: 01823 680233**

HEMYOCK MOTORS
Hemyock,Cullompton,Devon.
MOT'S. SERVICING, CAR SALES
Andy & Geoff Perry Tel: 01823680591

Newcott Service Station : A303, Honiton - 01404 861547

P.S.MARSDEN SHEAFHAYNE GARAGE
(Sponsor Page 85) Sheafhayne Yarcombe.
BODY REPAIR SPECIALISTS : CAR SALES.
Telephone : 01460 67858/ 0860 879691

SPARKS GARAGE : Blagdon Hill, Taunton.
SUZUKI SPECIALISTS
PETROL SERVICING REPAIRS & RECOVERY.
(Sponsor Page 37) **Tel: 01823 421606**

STOPGATE SERVICE STATION
(Sponsor Page 3) At the A303/B3170 Junction
News, Groceries, Videos, Everything for Your Convenience
& Car - (See Page 89) - **Tel: 01404 861214/376**

Wellington Service Station. - Tel: 01823 662608
Yarcombe Garage, Yarcombe. - Tel: 01460 63199

GARDEN CENTRES & NURSERIES

Blackdown Nurseries, West Buckland. - 01823 661699
Chard Garden Centre, Cuttisfords Door - 01460 63088

F.J.Jackson & Son Ltd. COMBE RALEIGH
WHOLESALE PLANT SUPPLIERS - (Sponsors Page 73)
Bedding & Pot Plants for the Professional Grower & Gardening Clubs
Tel. **01404 42228** **Honiton** Fax. **01404 44933**

STREET ASH NURSERY

John Williams (R.H.D. Wisley)
COMBE ST. NICHOLAS
(Sponsor Page 15)
Tel : **01460 234582**

IER View Nursery, Dunkeswell. - 01404 891376
Nursery of Miniatures, Northcote Hill. - 01404 42617
Ward Alpines - Hemyock - 01823 680410

GARDEN ESSENTIALS

FLOWER BARROWS
JOHN BIMSON HEMYOCK
Hand Made Garden furniture
(Sponsor p9) 01823 680395

MORGAN GARDEN MACHINES
Service : Repair : Spares : New Machines
All Makes of Lawn mowers,Chain Saws & Strimmers
(Sponsor Page 11) : **Tel: 01823 667116**

David Garden Services - Uffculme - 01884 820837

David Meatyard - Garden Maintenance - 01823 421468

Nick Stevens - Compost and Manure - 01404 891684
PCS Garden maintenance - 01823 661750
Proctors Woodflakes - Garden Bark - 01404 891245
Terry Anderson - Garden design - 01460 234596
Trimmit & Strimmit : Garden Maintenance - 01460 234578
Ward Alpines, Hemyock. - 01823 680410
Willowbank, West Buckland. - 01823 461324

GENERAL HANDYMEN

M.J.Bradford, Hemyock - 01823 680414/0378 614949

HAY & STRAW FOR SALE

Churchstanton -No artificial ferts/sprays - 01823 601222
S.G.Trim - Big /Small Bales-Churchstanton - 01823 601295

HAIRDRESSERS

IMAGES : Fore Street : Hemyock - 01823 680531

VISIONS UNISEX HAIRDRESSERS 01404 891133
Highfield Shopping Centre - **Dunkeswell**

STRANDS UNISEX HAIR SALON : CULMSTOCK
***Personal Styling for your Hair* - 01884 840224**

SNIPPETS. **Sharon Morgan** Unisex Hairdresser
27 Station Rd. **Hemyock.** - **01823 680075**

Shirelys L & M's Hairdressing -Uffculme - 01884 841005

HEATING AND PLUMBING

C.B.S **PAUL CATLEY (Sponsor P89)**
HEATING & PLUMBING ENGINEER
Hole Farm : CLAYHIDON : 01823 680521

HEATING & PLUMBING

G.D Webb: Plumbing & Heating : Hemyock -01823 680773
RS Heating, Uffculme - 01884 841334 / 0860 927176

HAULAGE - LIVESTOCK & GENERAL

Kentisbeare - David Pengelly - 01884 266306
Churchstanton - S.G.Trim - 01823 601295

HEDGE LAYING

Gary Coombes - 01460 68666
John Coombes - 01935 863207
Richard Ball - Forestry Contractor - 01823 664553
C.J.Barrow -Agri-Contractor - 01404 891510 / 0468 025274
David Lock - Agricultural Contractor - 4674 47121
Derek Webb Dulcis Farm Kilmington - 01297 33310

HEALTH

THE BLACKDOWN PRACTICE - **01823 680206**
AXMINSTER SURGERY, St. Thomas Crt - **01297 32126**

Diana Griffith MSSCH : MBCHA
CHIROPODY IN YOUR OWN HOME
Registered Member of the British Chiropody Association
(Sponsor p12) **For an Appointment Tel: 01460 67999**

Osteopath - Harvey Fudge DO, MGO. - 01823 680206

HORSES

EQUINE INSTRUCTION - HACKING - LIVERY

Curland Equestrian Centre, Curland - 01460 234234
Greenham Equestrian Centre, Wellington - 01823 673024

THE WELCOME CENTRE
CHRIS & JANE INVITE YOU TO ENJOY
* RIDING AT HEAZLE STABLES
* VISITOR INFORMATION & CAFE
* EVENTS IN HEAZLE ARENA
(Sponsor P 41) TELEPHONE 01823 680280

LIVERY & FACILITY

Sheldon Equestrian Centre - Blackborough - 01823 681118

Hilary's Horse Hotel, Buckland St. Mary - 01460 234460
A HORSE HOTEL ONLY - for that special equine break

Maxine Watson M &S Livery Sponsor P 10
Georges Farm, West Buckland, Wellington **Prestige Livery Yard**
ALL REQUIREMENTS CATERED FOR. Large Gallops, Enclosed Sand School, Venue & Arena : **AVAILABLE FOR PRIVATE HIRE**
01823 662180 (Home) 01823 660760 (Stables)

The Irish Draught Horse Soc Newsletter & Sale list
Heather or Graham Chaplin - 01823 601372

SADDLERY

Philip Ireland **UNICORN SADDLERY**
HORSE FEEDS : WORMERS : ALMOST EVERYTHING FOR THE EQUESTRIAN.
Netherclay Farm, Thurlbear, Taunton.TA3 5AX
Sponsor Page 17 Tel : 01823 321753

INSURANCE CONSULTANTS

Culm Valley Insurance, Uffculme - 01884 840066

KITCHENS AND CABINET MAKING

Nut Tree Kitchens - Uffculme - 01884 840796

David Chappell
Kitchen Showroom & Workshops
AT WEST BUCKLAND
(Sponsor Page 35) Tel: **01823 662162**

LIVESTOCK

Oakleaf Herefords - Buckland St. Mary - 01460 234394
The Postlebury Flock of Pedigree Shetlands - 01823 601372
Joan Barton - Flock of Pedigree Shetlands - 01823 480663
Sunnyside Flock of Dartmoor Grey Face - 01404 43419

MUSIC

Country & Western -60's - Entertainers - Matt - 01823 601270

RESIDENTIAL AND CARE HOMES

Hemyock, Downmead Care Home,Hemyock-01823 680323

HOLLY BANK HOUSE
CHURCHINFORD
A Nursing & Residential Home on the Blackdowns
(Sponsor Page 1) : **Tel : 01823 601447**

FUELS & LUBRICANTS

Oilsure - Fuels & Lubricants - 01404 891130

PAINTERS & DECORATORS

A.J. Duddridge - Churchstanton - 01823 601239

Mr. F.W.C. Foxwell **FOXWELLS** (Sponsor p 69)
DECORATORS & GENERAL MAINTENANCE
CHURCHINFORD
TEL: **01823 601204**

Rodney Snow - Hemyock - 01823 681046
Ray Cavill - Uffculme - 01884 840727

PET FOOD

OSCAR PET FOOD : KATE HEALEY : 01404 46771

PHOTOGRAPHIC & VIDEO

Chapmans Processing: Galmington - 01823 256056
Martin Street Photography, Honiton - 01404 41182

SKYCAM PHOTOGRAPHY : ADRIAN THORNTON
Aerial Photography With Excellence : (See Page 18)
Dunkeswell Airfield - Tel 01404 891889

Moving Art *Videographers*
MULTI-CAMERA - SEMINARS - EVENTS - O B
COMPLETE SCRIPT TO SCREEN
BETA SP - *PRODUCTION FACILITIES* -MEDIA 100
01823 601679 -Sponsor Cover - 01278 450496

POTTERS & CERAMICS

D. Arkle, Pound House, Membury - 01404 881431
A Trimlett - Coldharbour Mill, Uffculme - 01884 841315
Cottage Tiles - Handmade tiles. - 01823 681018
Culm Valley Ceramics : Painting Tuition - 01823 680121

SEWING MACHINES

Ian Hooper, Service Centre - 01823 333007 / 601347

SCRAP METAL TRADERS

M.D. Corbin, Wylam House, Monkton - 01404 46020
Yarcombe Motor Spares - 01460 63189

POST OFFICES

Broadhembury Post Office & Stores - 01404 841201

Buckland St Mary Post Office Stores : Sponsor Page 27
William & Mrs Butt : **Groceries & Wines** : 01460 234225

Churchinford Post Office and Stores : Sponsor Page 46
COL/BW Photocopying :Grocery etc -Tel : 01823 601220

Clayhidon Post Office - 01823 680311
Combe St. Nicholas PO Stores - 01460 62106
Culmstock Post Office Stores - 01884 840232
Dunkeswell - Highfield Post Office Shop - 01404 891986
Kentisbeare Post Office & Village Stores - 01884 266225
Luppitt Post Office - 01404 891220

Membury Post Office and Stores : Sponsor Page 77
Pauline & Keith Jacobs Groceries,Wines,Cards 01404 881225

Stockland Post Office - 01404 881220
Yarcombe Post Office - 01404 861598

PRINTERS

Impact Design & Typsetting - Luppitt - 01404 891296

THE COMPLETE PRINTING SERVICE ALL UNDER ONE ROOF
ON THE A303 NEAR CHARD
Neil wells : Tel : 01460 234100
(Sponsor P22) : Fax : 01460 234797
Rapid Print

SHOPS

WILLIAM & MRS BUTT
BUCKLAND ST. MARY
POST OFFICE & STORES
Wines : Country Delicatessen : Groceries
(Sponsors Page 27) - Tel: 01460 234225

CHURCHINFORD POST OFFICE STORES
GROCERIES :WINES :STATIONARY : COLOUR & BW PHOTOCOPYING FAXING : NEWSPAPERS AND MAGAZINES
(Sponsors P46) **Faith & Martin Newman Tel: 01823 601220**

Foxwells Bakery - Churchinford - 01823 601203
Groceries " Baking for The Blackdowns" Fresh Produce

The Bungalow Stores- Combe St Nicholas -01460 62583
Combe St. Nicholas PO Stores -01460 62106
Culmstock PO Stores -01884 840232
Dunkeswell Highfield PO Shop, Dunkeswell -01404 891986

HIGHFIELD GARAGE & GENERAL STORE
Dunkeswell - John Winwood - 01404 891258

Hemyock Spar - Station Rd. Mrs Stephney - 01823 680408
Hemyock PO Stores - 01823 680259

THE POST OFFICE AND STORES AT MEMBURY
WINES, FRESH FARM PRODUCE, GROCERIES, NEWSPAPERS AND CARDS.
(Sponsors P 77) - Pauline & Keith Jacobs - Tel: **01404 881225**

HIGHLANDS FARM SHOP
DOROTHY & IVOR - SMEATHARPE - Sponsors p68
Fresh Fruit & Veg, Cream, Preserves, Plants & Composts - Eggs & Ice Cream
TELEPHONE : **01823 601296**

STOPGATE SERVICE STATION
(Sponsor Page 3) At the A303/B3170 Junction
News, Groceries, Videos, Everything for Your Convenience & Car - (See Page 89) - Tel: 01404 861214/376

RURAL CRAFTS

Martin Symes - Woodturner & Wheelwright - 01404 861340

SECURITY

Roy Price, Hemyock - 01823 680814 / 0385 752757

SEPTIC TANK CLEANING

P. Tucker - 01884 277256

SOLICITORS

Chris Wheeler - Ashill, Uffculme - 01884 840491

TAXIS

ALLENS TAXIS & Mini-Coaches : (Est. 1985)
21, Parklands, Hemyock, Devon.
"Based in the Blackdowns"
(Sponsor p88) Tel: 01823 680708

Cabline - 01404 43775 / 41411

TELEVISION REPAIRS

Rayner Services -Yarcombe - 01460 234452
WeMT.V. Wilf Milton - 01823 680777 / 0802 313970

THATCHERS

RICHARD BUTTERFIELD
MASTER THATCHER
Member of The Somerset Thatchers Association
(Sponsor P 75) **01823 421366 / 01460 66740**

Jason Duggan - 0468 645898
Inthatch, 'Wakeley' Otterford - 01460 234477
Carl Ward, Hemyock - 01823 680833

TIMBER MERCHANTS

Allan Bright, The Beacon, Monkton - 01404 43411
Fraser - Harris - Culmhead - 01823 421395
Peter Quinain English Hardwoods - 01404 891713 /0891291
Brookridge Timber Ltd. Hemyock - 01823 680546

TOY MAKERS

Forever
Dolls Houses & Miniatures
The Shop at Lyme Street.
Axminster, Devon
Tel: 01297 34429. (Sponsor p 76)

Sheafhayne Farm Toys - Yarcombe - 01460 66023

WATER

R&D Filtration - 01404 861386
South West Water - 0345 776677
Wessex Water - 0345 300600 * Billing - 085 6002600

WEAVERS

CULM VALLEY WEAVERS
CULM VALLEY WEAVERS ARE SPECIALIST COMMISSION WEAVERS CARPETS & WALLCOVERINGS
(Sponsors P 53) Tel: 01404 891898

WINDOWS & CONSERVATORIES

Churchills - Dunkeswell - 01823 680385
Country Window - Dunkeswell - 01404 891144/ 891147
Michael Courtney - Window Cleaner - 01404 891764
Pring & Son - Hemyock - 01823 680405
Redwoods - Clayhidon - 01823 680268 / 01823 680571

WINE

COURTMOOR WINES- Courtmoor Farm,Upottery
Quality wines at Reasonable Prices
Always a good selection available
Tel 01404 861565 : Fax 01404 861474

Buckland St. Mary PO Stores - 01460 234225
Churchinford PO Stores - 01823 601220
Dunkeswell - Highfield Stores - 01404 891986
Hemyock Spar - Station Rd. Mrs Stephney - 01823 680408
Membury Post Office and Stores - 01404 881225
VIGO : Vineyard Equipment Hemyock - 01823 680230

WELDERS

M.D.Fabrication, Horn Rd, Kentisbeare - 01884 266692

The Next Edition of This Publication will be released on 1 st. April 2002 : For those of you who will be interested in Sponsoring pages and / or advertising in the new edition please write to - ***Michael Drury-Beck at Litework Productions***
19 Fairfield Green, Churchinford, Somerset
TA3 7 RR. Tel/Fax 01823 601 679